uncon FAITH

EVERETT D. REAMER

unconquerable FAITH

Fly Paper Productions, LLC
Publishing Group
P.O. Box 324
Harrison, OH 45030 USA
(812) 637-6908
(812) 637-6883 Fax

[SAN No. 255-2485]

Everett D. Reamer
Unconquerable Faith

ISBN: 0-9724397-2-2 (soft cover)

Cover concept by Fly Paper Productions. Cover designed and created by John Windhorst of Hammerhead Graphix. Inside page illustrations and layout by John Windhorst.

For more information on available discounted pricing for bulk purchases of this book, please contact the publisher, Fly Paper Productions, LLC at the address shown above.

Some special notes for our readers...

The majority of the images appearing with this story were photographed approximately sixty years ago – many actually created by Japanese photographers. Although every effort has been made to provide quality images for the book, some photos may appear less than perfect by today's photographic standards. Each image has been digitally scanned for best results.

100% of the net proceeds from sales of this book are being donated to the Children's Learning Center for Dyslexia of Cincinnati, Ohio. The Children's Learning Center was established by the Supreme Council of 32° Masons headquartered in Lexington, Massachusetts. All services furnished by the Center are provided to enrolled children totally free of charge.

This book is dedicated to my dear, late mother who with my father and other family members endured many dark and uncertain days during the period of my enslavement as a P.O.W.

Everett D. Reamer

Acknowledgements

Firstly, I wish to thank my wife, Bernice Cole Reamer, for her patience, fortitude, and emotional support which was so critical during the long hours of preparation for this book and more importantly, her willingness to endure along with me the painful emotions and memories of a time of such horror that it can never be forgotten.

Special thanks go to my friends, Dr. John M. Cutter, whose generous talents and efforts brought my story to the public in its more readable form; Gary W. Puckett, for his assistance in publishing and distributing <u>Unconquerable Faith</u>; and, Charles A. Brigham, III, for his leadership role in the formation of the "Heroes of a Generation Class" reunion of the 32nd Degree Masons of the Valley of Cincinnati and his promotional help with this book.

Thanks also go to those friends and family who contributed documents and photos, which helped to refresh my memory.

I further wish to express my gratitude to President Harry S. Truman for his courageous decision to authorize the dropping of the atomic bombs. It brought about the end of the war and saved the lives of us POW's being held by Japan; it also prevented the need for an allied invasion on the Japanese mainland, which by estimation would have cost one million allied casualties; and, it prevented the Japanese from carrying out their orders to assassinate all POW's, if and when a land invasion began.

Thank you to our Allied Forces who put themselves in harm's way to attain a "full and absolute" victory by recovering all Allied prisoners held by the Japanese. Likewise, the prompt action of the U.S. Army's First Cavalry to recover me, and others, can never be forgotten. Likewise, the excellent medical attention we received saved many lives and allowed us to return to a normal life.

And, last, but not least, I want to thank my own family members who have tried to understand and have shown so much love and patience to me over the years.

It has been a rocky road – 40% of us POW's did not survive Japanese internment – and only a few of us are alive today; but, life is precious, and our great country is generous. God bless America!

Everett D. Reamer

Foreword

Before the men and officers inside Malinta Tunnel marched out to surrender to the Japanese on Corregidor, the Voice of Freedom radio service broadcast one last message to a listening world:

"Bataan has fallen. The Philippine-American troops on this war-ravaged and bloodstained peninsula have laid down their arms. With heads bloody but unbowed, they have yielded to the superior force and numbers of the enemy."

"The world will long remember the epic struggle that Filipino and American soldiers put up in the jungle vastness and along the rugged coast of Bataan. They have stood up uncomplaining under the constant and grueling fire of the enemy for more than three months. Besieged on land and blockaded by sea, cut off from all sources of help in the Philippines and in America, the intrepid fighters have done all that human endurance could bear."

"For what sustained them through all these months of incessant battle was a force that was more than merely physical. It was the force of an unconquerable faith – something in the heart and soul that physical hardship and adversity could not destroy! It was the thought of native land and all that it holds most dear, the thought of freedom and dignity and pride in these most priceless of all our human prerogatives."

"Bataan has fallen, but the spirit that made it stand – a beacon to all the liberty-loving people of the world – cannot fall!"

More than sixty years later, these words still resonate and underscore the unflinching commitment these men and boys accepted and shouldered as their undeniable responsibility and individual jobs in an effort to secure the freedoms we now enjoy today.

My first opportunity to become acquainted with Everett D. Reamer was in Boston, Massachusetts in September of 2000. Both of us, together with eight others, were present from Cincinnati, Ohio to receive our 33rd Degree from the Supreme Council of the Ancient Accepted Scottish Rite, a division of

Freemasonry. Very often, I'm asked why I'm a member of this fraternal and charitable organization. My answer is that I have had an opportunity to meet men from across the world who have been tried by life itself; and, because of their values, principles, commitments, and honor, are willing to be tried again, and again, and again.

Everett D. Reamer is just such a man. A boy who became a soldier who became a prisoner, he remained steadfast under the fire of war and then faced unspeakable brutality and privation only to become a man of the highest dignity, humility, and grace. Experiencing firsthand the abusive hatred of an enemy that showed no mercy to those they held captive, Everett has never allowed himself to be defined by the easy justification of being consumed by that same hate. Although still bearing the scars and physical consequences of repeated torture, he nevertheless leads a life which is robustly positive, happily active, and which keeps its eye on the future.

It is no small exaggeration to say that the world we enjoy today is due primarily to the men and women of Everett's generation. At an average age of 22, they were called upon to protect democracy and freedom during one of its darkest moments. They did so without hesitation, answering that same call, while sacrificing the comforts of home, family, and safety, even to the point of making the ultimate sacrifice of life itself. It is not given to everyone to bear arms for their nation's defense. But, we who have reaped the benefits of what they have so unselfishly provided us must be profoundly and forever grateful. For, upon their return to peace, having seen the destruction of war, they sought to build; having seen inhumanity and suffering, they sought to heal; and, having seen the chaos of a sanity run amuck, they sought to return order, justice, and governance that would benefit all people.

Of the 36,000 American men and women who fought on Bataan, Corregidor, and the Philippine Islands, only 2,000 are living today. I'm certain that each, like Everett Reamer, has a story to tell. And, if it were possible, we should be bound to hear each of those stories. For, in a time and era when our nation again is at war in Afghanistan and Iraq, it is prudent to remember what others have faced in an effort to preserve the spirit of liberty, the freedom of the individual, and the personal dignity of humankind.

Today as yesterday, the words of President Harry S. Truman are relevant as we face the difficult and painful role of our world responsibility:

"...We are a people who not only cherish freedom and defend it, if need be with our lives, but we also recognize the right of other men and nations to share it...We must act ahead of time to stamp out the smoldering beginnings of any conflict or aggression that may threaten to spread over the world...Democracy is a matter of faith – a faith in the soul of man, a faith in human rights... (a) faith (which) gives value to all things; and without faith, the people perish..."

Like its nickname, Corregidor stands as "The Rock" upon which the memories of Everett D. Reamer and his fellow Allied soldiers now bind all us alike to the affirmation that freedom is truly never free; that our values are indestructible only so long as there are those who are willing to take action to preserve and defend them; and, that all too often these most precious of freedoms have been dearly paid for in blood. It is a story of personal courage. It is a story of unimaginable endurance. It is a story of the debt we owe to those who have stood fast to protect us. Indeed, it is a story of unconquerable faith.

John M. Cutter

1

Patriots Past and Present

*"It is foolish and wrong to mourn the men who died.
Rather we should thank God that such men lived."
– General George S. Patton*

*"You know the real meaning of peace only if you have been
through war." — Kosovar*

Cleves, Ohio, was typical of small-town, rural America in the 1930's. My family had moved there from Elizabethtown nearby where I was born on January 20, 1925. My father, Walter E. Reamer, worked as a section hand for the New York Central Railroad until a disability would cause him to take a job as a Crossing Watchman. He married Alma Hall Reamer, who was homemaker and mother to my four brothers, my four sisters, and me. Even my maternal grandfather, James W. Hall, lived with us. Although the simplest of luxuries were scarce in those post-Depression days, we were rich in family as each night 12 members of the Reamer household would sit down together around the supper table.

One indispensable luxury that I was fortunate to have was my education. The teachers at both the elementary and high schools in Cleves were fantastic! Professional, disciplined, and demanding the best from us at all times, they knew that knowledge provided an invaluable key to unlocking the future of a rapidly changing world.

While in the fourth grade, I remember reading a copy of National Geographic in which an article appeared about the mining of uranium and its potential as a source of unlimited energy. Little did I know then how important that energy would be to my very survival!

All of this forged an undeniable independence in me at a very early age. At 9 years old, I began mowing lawns, husking corn in the fields, and filling coal bins for our neighbors. At 10, I added a newspaper route and delivered the "Cincinnati Post & Times Star" to homes in town. And, since no license was required in those days, by 13 years of age, I had learned to drive the family's 1931 Ford automobile. As I grew older, I included a part-time job helping out at the hardware store in town, as well as shining the shoes of the patrons of the local barber shop. The cost was 10 cents a shine.

Still, regardless of our age, or the jobs we held, all of us youngsters had an obligation to participate in the annual Memorial Day parade. We would assemble at the south end of Miami Avenue. From there, with bands playing and flags on our shoulders, we proudly marched the full distance to Maple Grove Cemetery for the culminating ceremonies. Just to the right of the cemetery's old, iron, gate entrance, we assembled at a small mound atop of which was a tall flagpole flying the American flag. Encircling the mound were a number of simple, white tombstones with the names and regiments of the Civil War veterans buried there. Silently they stood, resolute, as if forming one last defensive perimeter around the flag and freedom they had so deeply cherished.

During one of these ceremonies, I became aware of an elderly, gray-haired gentleman. Somewhat bent with age, he struggled to stand as he listened as the songs were sung and guns were fired by the Honor Guard; and, with tears in his eyes flowing down upon his cheeks, he gave homage to these Civil War veterans, as the last bugle call sounded. He knew in the depths of his inner being the sacrifices of those he had fought with, those he had fought against, and those who had died to save this great nation from an internal disintegration over slavery. He, along with others, answered the call of duty. They paid an overwhelming price. And, they learned that freedom is never free. It is paid for, and always shall be, by the men and women who are willing to fight and die to protect our security and freedom.

It was through these emotional experiences that I gained the respect and reverence for this country and all it stands for. I felt then that I knew why so many of my family and friends had answered the call to serve. My own Grandfather had fought in the Spanish-American War in 1898, and so many other family and friends had served in World War I, the "War to End All Wars". Sadly, Germany in 1932 and then Italy in 1938 would disagree with that characterization.

In 1940, war seemed imminent as the nation was in serious negotiations with Japan over trade issues and Japanese actions in China. Lend Lease was being considered for Britain and Russia to stave off Germany's onslaught in Europe. In addition, the U.S. government initiated the draft in order to build and maintain an adequate military force. Some of my friends volunteered. Others were drafted. I could not wait. I felt the duty and obligation to enter military service while I was still a sophomore at Taylor High School. The problem was my age: I wasn't 18 years old which was the minimum age one could enlist.

Because I knew how to drive, I had been helping my brother, Paul, with U.S. mail contracts. He would meet the trains, pick up the incoming mail, and deliver it to nearby towns. He would also pick up outgoing mail and deliver it to trains for shipment to other parts of the country. Now that Paul was attending college, I had taken over his contracts. This job gave me access to the Cleves train depot where my friend, Arthur Templeton, was station master and a notary public.

I talked the matter over with my friend, Robert Grant. Robert wanted to enlist too. So, we decided to wait until I turned 16. After my birthday in January of 1941, we traveled to the recruiting station at the Main Post Office in Cincinnati, Ohio. We talked with the recruiters and were given the necessary applications which required our parent's signature to verify our age. After returning home with our paperwork, Robert confided to me that he was backing out of our plan; but, I told him I was going through with it — with or without him.

My plan was simple: I had decided to add two years to my age; enlist in the army; and, contact my parents to tell them what I had done

Enlistees line up.

once I reached my assigned base. I completed all the U.S. Army regulation forms and painstakingly wrote *"Walter E. Reamer"*, my dad's name, on the signature line thus giving me permission to enlist at the age of 18. There was only one more hurdle...my dad's signature needed to be notarized! So, in the early morning hours, with no one around the train, depot, I quietly went to where I knew Arthur, the station master, kept his notary stamp. Mission accomplished!

On February 2, 1941, without telling my parents, I took a bus back to the recruiting station in Cincinnati and joined up. I was taken to Fort Thomas, Kentucky, where I received my Army uniform and kit.

I was then housed in one of the barracks to await travel to my next destination which was California.

On February 6th, I was summoned to the command post at Fort Thomas. There to greet me were my father and a dear friend and mentor, Claude "Red" Downard, for whom I had worked in his barber shop. I was shocked! All my plans had apparently been discovered. If I could have disappeared as fast as Houdini, I would have! But, it was Red who spoke up for me. He told my dad that, with my background and past experiences — the numerous jobs I had held; the fact that I had been driving and handing the mail contracts for my brother; and my having learned teamwork while being part of the basketball and football teams in high school — he should let me go. And, with that, and a little more encouragement from Red, my dad finally agreed to officially sign me into the U.S. Army and advance my age by two years to 18. That night, I was permitted to return home to bid farewell to my family and friends. The following day, my uncle, Orville Hall, drove me to Cincinnati, Ohio for my official swearing in to the U.S. Army.

In mid-February of 1941, I and six other recruits were transported by train on a Pullman car to San Francisco, California. When we reached the docks, we were ferried out into the Bay to Fort McDowell on Angel Island. From here, I awaited transport to the Philippines, the duty destination I had specifically chosen.

While stationed here, I had opportunities to visit Oakland and the Bay area. I also had the chance to visit my aunt, Ida Atteberry. Her husband had died in a construction accident while building the Golden Gate Bridge; and, Ida then devoted her life to missionary work in the Mission District of San Francisco. At times, I would travel with her to her various assignments and services. She was an excellent communicator and a woman of unshakable faith.

US Army Transport ship
– *Republic*

On March 31st, shouldering my gear, I marched onto the gangway of the *USAT Republic*. As I boarded, a soldier with a clipboard looked at me and said: "Name and serial number." "Reamer, Everett D., # 15065691," I replied. After settling in, I watched as we passed under the Golden Gate Bridge and departed San Francisco Bay. I was assigned to a stateroom with another recruit by the name of John Perkowski. Even more posh, I took my meals in the formal dining room. In this ball-room-like setting with a spiral staircase, our tables were served by Filipino waiters. Was I dreaming? Surely, heaven had smiled on me! My first train ride across the broad American landscape in a Pullman car, and now luxury accommodations on the Republic on my way to a tropical island. Boy, this Army life was great! First class all the way!

Topside Barracks
(1941)

Corregidor *(looking west)*

By April 6th, we had docked at Honolulu, Hawaii. I was disappointed, however, not to be permitted off the ship to visit as we were supposedly quarantined. The next day, refueled and re-supplied, we were back under steam. Finally, on April 20th, we arrived at

Manila in the Philippine Islands. The scenery was spectacular. Under a brilliant sun, the jungle's mountains met the open sea in a cascade of deepest greens. We tied up at Pier 7, and it didn't take long before we were transported to the island of Corregidor by ferry. The island

Middleside Barracks
(current day)

itself was an afterthought of a landmass – only 1,800 acres in all. As we entered Corregidor's docks, I could see some soldiers on shore. They seemed to be yelling something at us. At last, their shouts could be heard loud and clear: "Suckers! Suckers!"

We were assigned barracks at Middleside, on the north end of Corregidor. Concrete structures with three floors, each unit had a mess hall, day room, cold water showers, and officers' quarters on the first floor. The second and third floors were set aside as quarters for the troops. With approximately 120 other men, I was assigned a bunk on the second floor. It was from there that I would often write to my family and friends back home via the Clipper mail service. Not long after my arrival, I received a package from the States. Opening it, I found a New Testament Bible that was encased in a zippered, khaki jacket and sent by my Aunt Ida. On the inside cover, she had written an inscription urging me to read certain scriptures which would help me find peace and hope whenever I felt lonely or in despair.

The following day, basic training started. This had been our very first training since enlisting Stateside. We were divided into four platoons with four squads to each platoon. Each platoon had an experienced Sergeant and officer assigned to it; and, each squad had assigned an experienced Corporal. For the next three weeks, our routine would be to fall out in front of our barracks at 0600 hours

(6 a.m.) each morning for calisthenics. We would then wash up for breakfast; and, at 0700, we would start our foot and movement training. The weather was oppressively hot and humid as we would hike.

Wheeler Battery

On the fourth week, we were issued our rifles and gas masks. Cleaning my rifle of its cosmoline protective grease and learning its serial number, I spent the next six weeks in extensive, restricted training. By the end of this time, I could field strip and reassemble my rifle without thinking, as well as knowing how to use my gas mask. From here, we went to training on the firing range and also did close encounter bayonet practice. By the end of the eighth week, we were declared fit and ready for hand-to-hand combat.

I also trained with Battery B 60th Coastal Artillery Anti-Aircraft. This unit split up and on June 1, 1941 was assigned to the newly formed Battery F 60th CA AA. In addition to the new recruits, Battery F's composition included original Battery B personnel who were seasoned soldiers and therefore the designated leaders of the newly formed unit. I became a fuse range setter on our 3 inch anti-aircraft gun. And, as an infantryman, I trained in the use of a Browning Automatic Rifle, or BAR as it was known.

In August, Battery F got its first taste of field position life. Manning Battery B's war position at Topside, near Battery Wheeler 59th CA, we were put on war alert status. For the entire four-week period we were at our posts, it rained continuously. I had seen rain in Ohio from the gentle showers of the spring, to the summer rains that the wind cascaded in visible sheets across the open fields, to the sudden and violent thunder storms of late July. But, this was a rain that was a constant, unrelenting, seemingly unending, monotonous downpour. We were drenched! Still, the hardworking background of my youth gave me the knowledge and the will to compete with those older than I in my battery. I never felt less because of my age, nor did I feel superior. Moreover, I never confided to anyone that I was only 16. Even to this day, my war record is that of an 18 year old and is permanently and proudly recorded on the records of time.

After returning to Middleside in September, we started intense training on our equipment that had just arrived. The equipment consisted of four M-3 anti-aircraft guns on M-2 A2 mounts, an M-4 director, two power plants, and an M-1 height finder. Battery F's code name was FLINT. We were an excellent anti-aircraft battery – of that I was sure! And, what about me? I was ready!

During this period, I had the chance to grab a leave or two. Below Bottomside, there was a shanty business district where Chinese tailors were

AA Battery Gun Drill

more than happy to make our khaki or blue denim uniforms for $3.00 — $5.00. I also visited Manila and mingled with the Filipinos, their markets and housing. It was certainly primitive; but, the people were always very friendly.

We had been scheduled to move from Corregidor to Bataan peninsula for our war time position. A drill and target practice position was organized on Cheney Point, just northwest of Battery Cheney 59th

CA. At the latter part of October, instead of moving to Bataan, we were ordered at the last minute to organize a war time position at this very practice position on Cheney Point. We started digging in for our gun emplacement. The soil was rain-soaked, hard, clay with large boulders. Yet, by mid-November of 1941, we had accomplished our task.

On the night of November 28th at 2100 hours, our Battery Commander, Major Glassburn, excitedly ordered us from our barracks on Middleside. "Japanese warships are on the high seas!" he said. "They may strike the Philippines!" All units on Corregidor were ordered to take up battle positions. As the next day dawned, Battery FLINT was in its field position on Cheney Point. Fifty rounds of M-3 ammunition were issued to each gun; 1,000 rounds more were received and placed in reserve in trenches dug approximately one year before by Philippine Scouts 92nd CA for 155 magazines. This area on the edge of the cliff overlooking the China Sea became our munitions storage area throughout the war; and, because it had been so strategically placed, it was never hit by enemy bombardment.

Crews fighting fires
(Pearl Harbor)

We were ordered to fire on all planes failing to follow certain routes or failing to follow certain recognition signals. Several times during the period between November 29th and December 8th, FLINT received the message: "...Hostile Planes Sighted over Northern Luzon. All Units Alerted..." With each message, our crews would spring into action as guns were manned and all instruments were powered up. Then, we would wait...and wait. The uncertainty labored against us. Still, every day at

USS Arizona attacked at Pearl Harbor

1200, a recording of Kate Smith singing "God Bless America" would come over the radio and lift morale for us all to a high level.

About 0430 hours on December 8, 1941, Battery F was again alerted. The message was the same as usual. You could hear the muttering and cursing: "These damned war games!"; "...can't get no sleep..." Then, at 0612 hours came the electrifying message, "Pearl Harbor attacked: Oahu bombed by Japanese planes at 0430 December 8, 1941 Philippine time. (December 7, 1941, Hawaii time): Battleships Arizona and Utah sunk: President Roosevelt has announced that a state of war exists between the U.S. and Japan." Even after this announcement, there were a few doubting Thomases that clung to the belief that it was all maneuvers.

All doubts were settled by turning on a radio. Huddled together in a tent as the rain fell underscoring the gravity of

FDR *Day of Infamy* speech

his words, we listened to President Roosevelt's address to Congress:

"Yesterday, December 7, 1941 – a date which will live in infamy – the United States of America was suddenly and deliberately attacked by naval and air forces of the empire of Japan.

The United States was at peace with that nation and, at the solicitation of Japan, was still in conversation with its government and its emperor looking toward the maintenance of peace in the Pacific.

Indeed, one hour after Japanese air squadrons had commenced bombing in the American island of Oahu the Japanese Ambassador to the United States and his colleague delivered to our Secretary of State a formal reply to a recent American message. And, while this reply stated that it seemed useless to continue the existing diplomatic negotiations, it contained no threat or hint of war or of armed attack.

It will be recorded that the distance of Hawaii from Japan makes it obvious that the attack was deliberately planned many days or even weeks ago. During the intervening time, the Japanese government has deliberately sought to deceive the United States by false statements and expressions of hope for continued peace.

The attack yesterday on the Hawaiian Islands has caused severe damage to American naval and military forces. I regret to tell you that very many American lives have been lost. In addition, American ships have been reported torpedoed on the high seas between San Francisco and Honolulu.

Yesterday, the Japanese government also launched an attack against Malaya.

Last night, Japanese forces attacked Hong Kong.

Last night, Japanese forces attacked Guam.

Last night, Japanese forces attacked the Philippine Islands.

Last night, the Japanese attacked Wake Island.

And, this morning, the Japanese attacked Midway Island.

Japan has therefore undertaken a surprise offensive extending throughout the Pacific area. The facts of yesterday and today speak for themselves. The people of the United States have already formed their opinions and well understand the implications to the very life and safety of our nation.

As Commander in Chief of the Army and Navy, I have directed that all measures be taken for our defense.

Always will our whole nation remember the character of the onslaught against us.

No matter how long it may take us to overcome this premeditated invasion, the American people in their righteous might will win through to absolute victory.

I believe I interpret the will of the Congress and of the people when I assert that we will not only defend ourselves to the uttermost, but will make it very certain that this form of treachery shall never again endanger us.

With confidence in our armed forces, with the unbounding determination of our people, we will gain the inevitable triumph. So help us God.

I ask that the Congress declare that since the unprovoked and dastardly attack by Japan on Sunday, December 7, 1941, a state of war has existed between the United States and Japanese Empire."

2

An Alamo One Hundred Times Over

"Success is not final, failure is not fatal: it is the courage to continue that counts." – Winston Churchill.

"Courage is fear holding on a minute longer."
– General George S. Patton.

With the President's words still ringing in our ears, bombing could be heard from the direction of Manila. Nichols Field and Cavite were bombed at about 0300 hours on the morning of December 9th.

Cavite in flames *(12/08/41)*

Smoke from these bombings billowed skyward and could be seen from our Corregidor positions.

Battery F fired its first shots of the war on the morning of December 10, 1941 (December 9th in the U.S.). For many of us, this was the first 3-inch anti-aircraft rounds the men ever fired or had even seen fired. The targets were several flights of Jap heavy bombers, the twin-tailed Mikado types, flying west over the North Channel between Bataan and Corregidor. These planes were within fuse range for only about three seconds. A 3 inch shell was placed in my fuse setter, and I set the fuse.

The rally man grabbed my shell and placed it into the gun breach. The gunner shoved the shell into the breach and locked it. "FIRE!!" came the command, as the gunner pulled the lanyard and our emplacement roared to life. It was about 15 seconds before the cease fire order was given. During that time, 27 bursts by our four guns were put up. "Our first war-firing experience," I thought to myself. "Not bad for green gun crews!" Although no damage to enemy planes was observed, the firing had the desired effect — we weren't gun shy anymore. However, it was during this initial firing that all of us realized the extreme inadequacy of our 21-second powder train fuse. Enemy planes flew over us and beyond our range. Battery B kept on putting bursts right in there with 30-second mechanical fuses. The envy we felt for Battery B's firing superiority was soon supplanted by a feeling of helplessness as flight after flight of enemy planes continued to bomb us from altitudes we could not reach. Nevertheless, Battery F showed coolness in action that day when they did not fire their small arms in frustration at the high flying enemy planes as many others did.

At the declaration of war, Battery F had four 3-inch guns in pits, so that when at zero degree elevation, all parts were below ground level — the range detector, height finder, power plants, communication center. The four local AA machine guns were in pits which had been evacuated by Battery I, a machine gun battery. Sandbags were very scarce since the only sand available was on the beaches at the far end of the island. To offset this deficiency, we used metal 12 in. and 155 mm propelling charge canisters filled with earth. All personnel were in tents; and, later in gun pits or at Battery Cheney. Electricity was available from Battery Cheney's 25 kW plant as well as from the post powerhouse system. Trees were topped to give a better field position for observation and height-finder equipment as was the growth cleared from around the area of our four 3-inch guns.

From December 10-29th, all was peaceful at Corregidor, but activity was intense. Jap bombers were seen daily. The bombing of Cavite was plainly audible and smoke was visible. Our ongoing challenge was to make our pits safe and more secure.

The Battery's Filipino hired hands remained around Battery Cheney and our height-finder crew's area. They worked as KP's, barbers, shoe shiners, and latrine orderlies. Their pay was 21.50 pesos ($10.25) per month with no other benefits provided for them or their dependents. They became close to the officer staff and worked faithfully throughout the bombardment with no defections. They all knew that their families were in Jap-occupied territory.

Japanese fighter planes over Corregidor

Standing in line for chow at approximately 1200 on December 29th, I looked skyward as the air raid sirens blew. The sirens had been heard many times in the preceding three weeks. Our air warning radar could detect planes 99 miles away, but the enemy had always given the island a wide berth. The Jap plane formations coming from the west straight toward Corregidor told me this time was going to be different. We quickly abandoned the chow line, ran to our guns, and started firing at the incoming planes. As bursts of anti-aircraft fire appeared, I heard a swishing sound followed by thunderous explosions as the first bombs hit Corregidor.

Our Battery Commander, Major Glassburn, was not at the position when the first flight came over. Instead, it was our range officer, Captain Bryan, who took charge and put us into action. Major Glassburn arrived as the second flight of planes came in for the attack.

The exact number of planes ranged from 54-81 of the heavy bombers and about 18 low-flying light bombers. The low-flyers flew a course from Battery Wheeler 59th CA directly over Batteries Cheney and FLINT. As they strafed us, our machine gunners fired back. Two planes were hit and fell into the sea. Wave after wave, the planes in tight formations continued their bombing. The ground around us shook as I set the fuses on the shells passed to me and passed them on in turn to be fired by our crew. Suddenly, a bomb fell within 10 feet of our # 3 gun, showering the area with fragments and knocking it out of action as shrapnel pierced the counter recoil cylinder. Its crew came running into our pit for cover, two of them wounded. Echoingly, thunder answered thunder as bombs fell and our gun bursts filled the skies.

Three and one-half hours later, the All-Clear sounded. I looked out of our pit as FLINT took stock of the damage. Not one man under fire had run or left his position! More than 30 bomb craters pockmarked our area. The water had been cut off in all pipes; cables had been cut; and, the post power lines were out of service. We had fired 254 rounds of 3 inch shells engaging nine flights of planes as we did. Several heavy bombers were reportedly shot down, but none were claimed by FLINT as it was impossible to distinguish the burst of any one particular Battery from those of another.

During this entire action, the Southwest Bunker (SWB) was located in a tent near Battery Cheney, near the director pit. It had no splinter proofing of any kind. When the dust cleared, the two operators were found working on the ground surrounded by foot lockers. Communication between FLINT and Red Battery F 1st BN 60 CA had gone out once before and had been restored there and also between the control position and guns by the Battery Communication

Section while the bombing attack was still in progress. These men received the Silver Star for their brave performance and several of them had Oak Leaf Clusters added because of their having repeated these acts a second time during the January 2nd bombardment of Corregidor.

Before we knew it, it was chow time. The cooks and KP's served a good hot supper, but there was too much excitement for appetites to be anything other than slim. I, like all of the men, came to

respect and admire the kitchen crews. No shelling or bombing ever prevented them from feeding the men. There were delays at times due to action, but we always got two meals a day.

Field Mess

All was quiet again on Corregidor. The Communication Section moved the SWB into the slit trench that ran under the concrete floor of the director emplacement and started a pit that was to become their regular post of operations during action.

On December 22, 1941, 50,000 Japanese landed and quickly overran Manila. With approximately 25,000 Americans under his command, General Douglas MacArthur had only begun to train 100,000 green Filipino recruits. Cut off from stores of weapons and supplies, General MacArthur ordered the bulk of our forces to withdraw along Manila Bay into the mountainous Bataan Peninsula north and west of the city. There amid rice paddies and volcanic terrain, he hoped to fight a delaying action until promised reinforcements and supplies could arrive. Unfortunately, the promises were only that because of the War Department's White House mandate to direct men

Filipino guerillas

Generals MacArthur &
Wainwright

Japanese troops landing
on P.I. *(12/16/42)*

Japanese tanks on road to Manila
(01/02/42)

Manila's damage following
invasion

Twelve-inch gun

and material to defeat Nazi Germany first. Manila was evacuated by December 31st as MacArthur advised his HQ and staff to retreat to   Corregidor, a mere 30 miles away.   From this evacuation,

we welcomed a platoon of U.S. Marines under Lt. James Keene. Although they arrived at 2030 hours of that same night, all of its 50-caliber machine guns were in position near the range finder area on navy deck mounts set in concrete by 2330. Pretty fast work on a dark night in strange terrain!

Battery Hearn open fires

This platoon lived, work, and fought side-by-side with F Battery until April 25th when it was moved to a new position to protect Battery Hearn 59th CA at Topside.

On January 2, 1942, the enemy bombing raids started again and continued until January 6th. The low-flying bombers were absent, and the heavies started increasing their altitude. They came at the same time every day, 1245

Battery Way emplacements

hours. Although many hits were scored in Battery F's area, the only damage they did was the cutting of one cable, knocking out telephone lines, and ruining tents and much of the clothing of the range section and gun crews. By the end of these four days of bombing, the men, including myself, were "well-salted". The bombing no longer affected appetites. The Japanese continued to lose from 5-15% of their aircraft on each bombing raid. Several more men were wounded, but only one had to be hospitalized. Corporal G. D. Smith was struck on the head by a large rock. His helmet saved his life.

Each day, the enemy flew higher, finally breaking from our range. Nevertheless, most flights could be reached by Battery B — the only battery with the 30-second mechanized fuses which had been brought in by submarine. As a result, the Japanese continued to lose planes. I knew just how much they respected our fire power because not once did any of their warships ever attempt to enter Manila Bay.

On January 7th, everyone was at his battle station at 1230 hours. Waiting I looked at my watch: 1235...a shell was passed to me for our first firing... 1240...we tensed ready to spring into action...1245...the anticipated moment we all knew to expect came and went...still no bombers appeared! The skies remained strangely empty as we continued to wait. It is no exaggeration to say that afternoon was the longest of the war. The next day was the same. A few heavy bombers appeared on January 14th, but none came within range.

During this time, we had an opportunity to affect repairs. The armored cables leading to our areas were frequently cut by bombs and shell fragments, and we turned them over to the ordinance crews for splicing. On one such day, I was ordered on a detail to the Topside ordinance shop. John Mai, another guy from our battery, was also being sent with us to an observation area near Battery Way 59th CA. We gave John a ride to Topside and after dropping him off, we continued on to the ordinance shop, which was located in the side of a hill. After we unloaded our cables to be repaired, our orders were to go to Bottomside to get water to fill some 12 inch metal powder containers we had brought with us for that purpose. I climbed onto the bed of the truck as we began backing out from the ordinance shop. "Too bad you guys have to work so hard today," taunted a GI outside the shop as he upturned an empty bottle of San Miguel beer.

Suddenly, bombs dropped through the cloudy sky all around us! Flashes of light filled my eyes as explosions seemed to rain down on top of us. The concussion was horrendous and made my head feel as if it were bursting open! My buddies and I dove for the ground as the driver dove under the still moving truck. The truck, tires and all, blew apart totally destroyed! Finally, there was silence. When I looked up, all but two of my buddies on the truck were lying across the road dead. Many more men around the ordinance shop were also killed. I looked at my hand which was stinging and found only a small wound there. I could barely believe how lucky I had been! After helping at the scene, the two other survivors from our detail and I walked back to our position on Cheney Point. As we came into view, we were greeted by cheering comrades. "Great to have you back, Reamer!" someone cried. "Heard you boys had bought the farm up on Topside!" shouted another. Shocked, I replied, "Not yet...not yet!"

All continued quiet. We improved splinter proofing and laid mine cable in place of rubber covered cable. Some of us built dugouts to our gun pits in anticipation of the rainy season. Most were never used. Poker, pinochle, and bridge occupied the longer hours of waiting. Radios were also very popular. Our group had a short wave on which we listened to the news from around the world. One day, I heard a reporter observe: "...give the Japanese enough rope, and they will hang themselves..." "Enough rope!" I thought to myself, "Doesn't this guy know we're the ones with our necks in the noose?"

On February 3, 1942, the Japanese attempted to land troops on the west coast of Bataan behind our lines. Battery Cheney ordered Battery F to take cover while they fired their 12 inch guns directly over our position toward the west coast of Bataan. Shell after shell whistled through the air thwarting the Japanese plan to take over Bataan by splitting our forces there. This was a major set-back for the Japanese.

About mid-February, Jap artillery in place on Cavite and Batangas opened fire on Fort Frank which was a short distance from the southern Luzon shore. Clearly visible from our battery position, the artillery duel between the Jap's artillery on shore and that of Fort Frank's and Fort Drum's was watched with great intensity. For several days, it had been generally believed that the Jap land artillery did not have the range to reach Corregidor. This impression was rudely reversed when the same guns started registering on Fort Hughes and then onto our area. One morning as we were waiting in line to get breakfast, we were suddenly

Fort Drum

shocked when shells from Batangas landed near us. I was slightly wounded. Shells from this attack also fell into the North Channel. The heavy shelling of Fort Frank and Fort Drum (the concrete battleship) later on provided a spectacle that the men of Battery F will never forget. On one particular day, the Japs

Voice of Freedom

dropped over 1,200 shells on Fort Frank. It seemed impossible that any of their guns could still be in firing condition. But, we were proven wrong when Fort Frank began to return fire after the enemy barrage let up. Later, we in FLINT learned something of the pressure the men on Fort Frank had endured.

All remained quiet as far as we were concerned. Water pipes were repaired and electricity was restored making radios popular again. All of Corregidor was put on half rations. Food was adequate right to the end. However, there were no fresh fruits, vegetables, butter, milk, eggs, or potatoes. At this point, rice became our staple. We also had canned spinach and some canned meat. Perishable foods had stopped with the destruction of the cold storage plant in March, except for occasional issues of caribou and mule meat that had been slaughtered on Bataan. Cigarettes were issued to smokers as part of their rations. Pipe tobacco, chewing gum had not been available for some time. Toothpaste, toothbrushes, razors and blades were hard to get. Toilet soap was at a premium and the supply of laundry soap was almost gone by the time of our surrender.

On March 11th, General MacArthur received orders to leave Corregidor. He departed the island via the north docks on the motorized torpedo boat, PT-41 to take command of the Allied Australian Theatre at Brisbane. Upon his arrival, he radioed back vowing the now famous words, "I have come through, and I shall return."

On March 24th, several large flights were seen passing far south, apparently headed for the battle in the northeast. The lull was on except for an occasional chance shot at lone G-2 spy planes known as "Photo Joes". But, later on the same day, bombers appeared again. From this time forward, their tactics were different: they came in small groups, sometimes in pairs, from all directions and at all hours. Rarely did they fly low enough for us to give us a good shot at them. My battery and I continued to fire at them, unless their altitude was over 24,000 feet. A great deal of the firing was done at fuse settings of 21 seconds and over. This was done because observation of our fire seemed to indicate many bursts occurred beyond the fuse time setting, thus giving us additional reach at higher altitudes.

From March 24th until May 7th, Corregidor was visited daily by heavy bombers. The numbers in each attack varied, but on one day 85 heavy bombers dropped bombs on us. We had many close calls. One large bomb, either a delayed action or anti-personnel type, hit within 60 feet of the director emplacement, leaving a 20 foot wide crater, 12 feet deep. I saw two pyramid type tents littering the spot where they had been standing with all their contents shredded. Another bomb went into the ground 23 feet from the west corner of the director emplacement and failed to explode. The wind from the pressure of its impact was felt by the height finder crew. Shortly after that, our crew was in their #3 pit position, when I became aware of a high pitched whistling sound heard high above the noise of our guns. "Hit the dirt!" someone yelled as a bomb burst so close by that it covered all of us and our equipment with debris. To this day, the sound of that explosion echoes in my memory.

After March 24th, bombs were dropped and exploded in mid-air above ground level – a cunning strategy as there was no overhead cover for us. In one raid, three of these air bursts occurred over our position. The concussion was quite heavy, but no one was wounded. Quite a few concrete-filled bombs landed in our battery area, but did no damage. Set with a sensitive fuse, we thought at first they were phosphorous. They left no crater, just a pile of powdered concrete. "Better shake that dust out of your hair," teased one of my gun crew. "The Japs like you red-heads best for pulling their rickshaws. "Needless to say, I didn't respond lightly to this kidding.

Two days later, at 1600 hours, our battery spotted two heavy bombers flying south to north over Corregidor at about 17,000 feet. Data was called in over the BN data net. One by one, all batteries reported on target. Battery F opened fire first, quickly followed by

Battery B, and then by other batteries. One of the first ten bursts chopped the right wing off one of the bombers. It spun down into the North Channel bay area in flames, its engines painfully screaming all the way. Cheering could be heard from both Corregidor and Bataan just two miles across the channel. What a boost to our morale! Although many planes had been downed previously, this was the first downing to disintegrate in plain view. The second plane crash landed into Manila Bay. Some pieces of that plane had dropped on land, were picked up, and brought to our battery for us to see. Never again did the heavy bombers fly low over Corregidor. They stayed above 21,000 feet.

Artillery night-firing
(On Bataan)

In late March, as the air raid warning sounded, a Private in our Battery from Somerset, Kentucky, was running to take cover at Battery Cheney. He toppled over the top of Battery Cheney's gun emplacement and landed some twenty feet below on the concrete floor in the pit. He died from his fall.

During the last week of March with the moon bright and full, the enemy tried night bombing. The search lights and guns picked them up so quickly and confused their aim so thoroughly that the raids became fewer and fewer each night. The raids resulted in minimal damage. Most of the bombs dropped were phosphorus and more than 50% hit in the water of the bay; none came near our battery.

Like a Fourth of July celebration, the exploding phosphorus bombs lit up like flower pot fireworks tracing the night in plumes of dazzling white, as the bursts of our anti-aircraft fire answered back with chrysanthemums of red and orange. About April 1, 1942, the attacks on Corregidor diminished. As the Japs began to concentrate their air actions on Bataan and Mariveles, we had a front row seat from our battery's position. The ships there and the "Dry Dock Dewey" made a particularly attractive target, but were hard to hit as the Navy had submerged it. The Navy ship, Canopus, a service and sub support ship, was eventually scuttled before the fall of Bataan. The sound of artillery fire on Bataan, both ours and theirs, increased in volume. It seemed to be getting worse every night. The sound and its flashes were like summer storms: thunder and lightening.

On April 8, 1942, the roar of the artillery on Bataan was incessant, the whole northwestern sky over Bataan lighted up. It was apparent that a heavy attack was being made on our lines. At about 2200, Battery Hearn 59th CA started firing 12 inch projectiles toward Bataan at two minute intervals. Sleep was impossible. The ammunition dumps' exploding caused such confusion that some thought earthquakes were occurring. It was clear that the Japs had broken through our last line of defense on Bataan and were now on the Cabcaben Road. At dawn, the whole southern end of the Bataan peninsula was covered with fires. Boats were used to transport men and equipment from Mariveles to Corregidor to avoid capture. Some managed to escape Bataan in bangkas (a type of Filipino outrigger canoe) and on make-shift rafts. Some swam all

General King

the way to Corregidor; many died before reaching us. In spite of all these obvious signs of defeat, it was a bitter blow to us to learn that General Edward King, Commander of Forces on Bataan had surrendered to the Japanese at 0800 hours on April 9, 1942.

Battery F received two men from the 200th CA and nine from the 515th CA (AA) during the night of April 9th. These men had escaped from Bataan with nothing but the clothes on their backs. In spite of the experience they had been through, they pitched right in and worked with us until we later had to surrender.

The Japanese thought that the Philippines would be a cake walk. After all, this was the same fleet which just a few short months ago had wreaked havoc on Pearl Harbor. By their estimates, the entire island grouping was to have been brought under control by no later than February. Those captured would be the first to feel the

Newspapers reporting fall of Bataan

Bataan *Death March*

Captives along the death march

Death march wounded in makeshift litters

Death marchers carrying the wounded

Slit-trench on Corregidor

Japanese Leaflets dropped
on Corregidor

wrath of General Masahura Homma who was first in Japanese Command. The day following their surrender, 70,000 Allies – about 14,000 Americans, the remainder Filipinos – were force marched from Mariveles to Camp O'Donnell 65 miles away. By the time they reached their destination 4 days later, heat, exhaustion, disease, starvation, and indiscriminate murder would result in the extermination

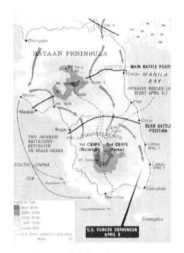

Map of fall of Bataan

of nearly 20,000 men. In the first 40 days after the Bataan Death March, another 1,500 Americans would die; and, by July, 25,000 more Filipinos would perish.

The Japanese artillery at once moved their batteries and directed their sights at Corregidor. Starting on April 10th from the vicinity of Cabcaben, light batteries opened fire on Corregidor, but none of the shells fell near us. Although our future looked uncertain at best, we maintained our courage and kept our hopes up. On the night of April 12th, a dive bomber came in right over our position with its running lights on. Every machine gun in range opened fire. The resulting display of machine gun tracers was impressive, even to the Jap observers on Bataan. Within 10 minutes after our machine guns had ceased firing, a 105 mm battery of Jap field artillery opened fire on the Cheney area and our Battery F. The salvos continued at the rate of about 5 per minute for 3 or 4 minutes. The fire was not only rapid but deadly accurate. The first salvo mortally wounded Private C. P. Greer, a U.S. Marine, by setting fire to the sleeping shelter he was in and destroyed the machine gun he had been firing. The Mess and Supply Sergeants left the shelter of Battery Cheney that was a haven for our height finder and general staff crews, and, in a valiant effort to save his life, pulled Private Greer from the burning shelter despite the heavy shelling and exploding 50-caliber ammo. Private Greer lived only a few minutes after he was brought to the area aid station at Cheney. Both the Mess Sergeant and Supply Sergeant received the Silver Star for their act of bravery. The shelling set fire to all the grass and brush in the Battery F area. Like all the others around me, I had to turn to and put out these fires. This was essential to prevent the ammunition and reserve gas from exploding. The gun crews normally stayed with their guns and not at Battery Cheney. At mess time, the gun crews would alternate to Cheney for chow once at dawn and once at dusk.

After the fall of Bataan, our field position was barren. The shells and bombs destroyed the dugouts and scalped the landscape like a GI haircut. It was decided that we would move our position at Cheney Point to a position near to Battery Hearn. I was delighted to help dig gun pits at our new location. One evening when we had dug down about 4 feet and were waist deep in our pit, we heard our 144 cut loose from near by. We kept digging though. Then, suddenly, the Japs on Bataan started shelling and seemed to have us dead in their sights. Shells dropped all about us as flashes lit up the sky. Everyone ran for cover, but four of us dropped in our tracks. While the others got to safety, I was hit in the back with fragments. We stopped digging, and it was decided by Major Glassburn that we would not move to this location. We ended the battle for Corregidor on Cheney Point.

About mid-April, the air raid siren had sounded and we were under shell fire from Bataan. Planes were approaching from the west in force. A #2 gun crewman, Private Paul E. Newsome, got out of our gun pit and started to run. Our gun Sergeant, Steve W. Milton, pulled out his 45-caliber sidearm and pointed it at Newsome as he ran. Three men of our crew restrained Sergeant Milton from shooting Private Newsome in the back. After this incident, Private Newsome returned and was a dedicated #2 gun crewman.

Battery F and Cheney with its two 12 inch disappearing coastal guns became closely united. Our men that were off duty were permitted to rest and sleep at Cheney. Messes were also now consolidated. Battery Cheney was short on manpower, whereas Battery F with the influx of extra manpower from other areas like Bataan, and also having #3's gun crew whose gun had been knocked out of action, gave us ample manpower to supplement them.

Sometime later in April, #2 gun crew was waiting to be relieved to go to breakfast mess at Battery Cheney. As we were relieved, I departed the gun pit into the trench that passed by a machine gun emplacement. I heard a shot and immediately yelled at the machine gunner, Private Harold Robeson. I then proceeded to his post to check out the reason for his firing the gun. I found him dead, his own 45 caliber automatic held to his chest. One of the crew of the #2 gun immediately notified Major Glassburn. He came, and we stated that we could not understand why Private Robeson wanted to take his own life. I was deeply shaken by this. Private Robeson had been my bunk buddy in barracks.

When Battery Cheney started to fire their 12 inch guns at targets on Mariveles, Battery F with its extra manpower was able to supplement and support the ammunition carriers and the rammer details. After the fall of Bataan, Battery G 60th CA was able to salvage two of their anti-aircraft guns from Bataan and bring them to Corregidor. Those of us in Battery F helped reconstitute Battery G providing equipment and supplemental manpower.

As soon as Battery Cheney started to shell targets on Bataan, the Japanese installed a 240 mm gun to the rear of Sisiman Bay. Without changing their azimuth, this gun gave direct access to Battery F, Battery Cheney, Battery Wheeler, and Battery Nonia. A battery of 150 mm guns was also assigned Battery Cheney as its primary target. On the second firing by Battery Cheney to targets on Bataan, both Jap units returned fire and registered hits all around Battery Cheney's two 12 inch guns. A direct hit was scored on the officers' sleeping shack. The shack was a total loss. The Japs then opened fire with their 150 mm on us. Any movement above ground was very risky. Our entire area was clearly visible from the hills of Bataan. From the start, our position had always been rather barren. But, after the bombing and shelling, we became a "no man's" land.

On a day in late April, our # 2 gun pit was being hit all around. I had stayed in the gun pit to take cover of the flying debris.

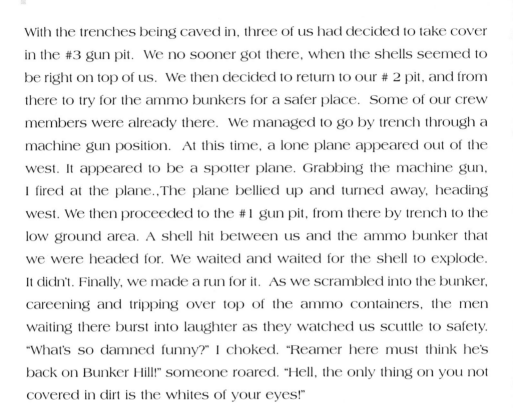

With the trenches being caved in, three of us had decided to take cover in the #3 gun pit. We no sooner got there, when the shells seemed to be right on top of us. We then decided to return to our # 2 pit, and from there to try for the ammo bunkers for a safer place. Some of our crew members were already there. We managed to go by trench through a machine gun position. At this time, a lone plane appeared out of the west. It appeared to be a spotter plane. Grabbing the machine gun, I fired at the plane.,The plane bellied up and turned away, heading west. We then proceeded to the #1 gun pit, from there by trench to the low ground area. A shell hit between us and the ammo bunker that we were headed for. We waited and waited for the shell to explode. It didn't. Finally, we made a run for it. As we scrambled into the bunker, careening and tripping over top of the ammo containers, the men waiting there burst into laughter as they watched us scuttle to safety. "What's so damned funny?" I choked. "Reamer here must think he's back on Bunker Hill!" someone roared. "Hell, the only thing on you not covered in dirt is the whites of your eyes!"

From Signal Hill and Mount Bataan, the Jap observers had open visibility to our vulnerable positions. Our Battery F had been without computer tracking abilities, due to severe damage to cables from our height finding center. To compensate, we spotted our target in azimuth and set the fuse clocks near 21 seconds. The guns were then elevated and fired until the plane targets were out of range. This was the signal for the Japs to open fire on us. When our Battery F crew would take cover in the gun pits, Jap shells would rain down on us.

Battery F Communication centered in the general area of our gun pits. In late April, after the fall of Bataan, our position on Cheney Point was a hot target for Jap shelling. The trenches would be caved in and dirt and debris flew all about. Private John Mai manning the gun communication center under the command of 1st Lieutenant Fred S. Dewey, Jr. found himself alone during one such hostile shelling. One always feels safer with another person. When the shelling let up, Lieutenant Dewey came to the Communication Center. "You take over," Mai said to Dewey, "I'm leaving". "You stand fast and maintain your post, soldier!" Lieutenant Dewey scowled. Private Mai disregarded the order and left his post. Before he could get too far, he was placed under detention and taken to Battery Cheney where he was held for court martial

From here on, the Jap artillery made our life a nightmare. The terrain looked like the surface of the moon. I dug a hole in the ground and in a wooden box I placed a set of clothes. Inside the shirt pocket I tucked the canvas-covered New Testament which had been given to me by my aunt in San Francisco just prior to my leaving for the Philippines. I rationalized that in case of invasion, I wanted a clean uniform to go into battle and my Bible protecting my heart.

Our cables continued to be frequently cut by shell fragments. It became necessary for all batteries to do their own splicing at night to keep the height finder data systems in operation. Quite often, near the end, we operated without the data systems and sighted our guns visually. Twice the gun pit ammunition was set on fire by exploding enemy shells. The platform on one gun was destroyed and replaced with a wooden deck. The gun was out of action until new data clocks could be installed. We had again attempted to haul water in the 12 inch metal powder cans. Bathing was reduced to a minimum. The cold storage plant was now permanently inoperable, as well as the post power plant. Fried bread made from cracked wheat flour was rationed at one slice per man per meal twice a day. When the post bakery was destroyed, our bread supply was stopped and hot biscuits were served once a day. Trucking water to the battery position daily was a very hazardous job. All delivery of supplies had to be done at night without lights as the enemy had a most unpleasant habit of interdicting with intermittent barrages on various roads.

Battery Hearn plotting-room

The dive bombers, absent around Corregidor since December 29th, now reappeared and tried day after day to hit Batteries Way and Geary 59th CA's 12 inch mortars. These two mortar batteries were doing excellent counter battery work against the Japs. Dive bombers usually carried a bomb under each wing, about 100KG in size. When flashing in dive bombers, all units had formed the habit of reporting whether or not they were carrying bombs. Our surprise was complete, when one of the dive bombers having no bombs visible, suddenly open up its bomb bay and released a stick of 7 bombs. These light bombers either had no bomb sights or ineffective ones. Their aim was not accurate. Still, they made a very difficult target for us; too low for 3 inch AA guns and too high for machine guns. Moreover, Corregidor's Fort Mills had no 37 mm AA material.

Corregidor 12" guns
fire on enemy
(May 1942)

During the last week of April, a direct hit by an artillery shell set our power plant motor on fire and destroyed our entire plant. Data clock and data cable damage by shell splinters kept our firing Battery FLINT down to only two guns in action at one time: #1 and #2 and these being fired by so-called "Kentucky windage", that is to say estimating azimuth, elevation, and fuse settings.

There were only two height finders left in working order. About 0200 hours on May 2nd, Battery F's height finder was removed and re-assigned to Battery B 60th CA AA as they were equipped with 30 second mechanical fuses and positioned at a higher elevation. Later in the morning of that same day, during a terrific barrage being laid down on our position, a 150 mm shell hit our height finder pit. We were overjoyed and congratulated each other that our height finder had been saved by its transfer to Battery B.

Meanwhile, the barrage continued and the whole island of Corregidor was shaken by a tremendous explosion. Battery Geary 59th CA's 12 inch mortar battery's powder magazine had been penetrated by an enemy shell and blew up. A column of dark smoke and dust rose over 3,000 feet above Corregidor. A chunk of concrete from Battery Geary about the size of a small dining room table had been blown some 1,050 feet horizontally and 120 feet vertically, landing at Battery B's 60th CA position, right on top of Battery F's height finder. By now, although it was evident to all of us that the end of our struggle was near, what the end would be was not so certain. No one wanted to talk about it. We continued to hope that help would come. We had no choice but to hope. I dreamed of ships on the horizon coming to our rescue. After Bataan fell, the order was "Corregidor can and will be defended." Some of us thought to ourselves that help would not and could not come in time. The mental strain was enormous, and many cracked under the constant shelling. The reason was easy to see: bombing you could understand. We had the answer for the planes that brought them. But, how do you answer the shellacking we were taking from shells that seem to come from nowhere and everywhere at once? It is highly laudable to all of us that the will to fight remained unabated.

From May 1st, our battery was on stand-by each night to move out as infantry to defend the beach defense positions. However, Battery F 60th CA was on last priority, so it was evident that an attempt to storm "The Rock" was expected. All of us believed that it would be defended to the last. Throughout the first days of May, the tempo of attacks increased daily, the artillery barrages grew heavier, and the bombers kept coming.

On the night of May 5th, the enemy artillery seemed to fire relentlessly. I had been on trench repair duty for a long period of time. I was to be relieved to get rest and spend the night inside Battery Cheney. No sooner then I had dozed off, an officer shook me: "Reamer! You go out and repair the trenches; I'll see you get a break tomorrow!" At about 2200 hours, Battery Cheney was ordered to move out for beach defense. We checked all our

Map of Bataan and Manila Bay

infantry armaments, machine guns, BAR's, ammunition, grenades, and stood by. There being a need for every able bodied soldier to man the lines, all charges against Private Mai were dropped; and, to his credit, he rejoined us to defend Sector B. It was apparent from the continuous rattle of machine gun fire and 75 mm. salvoes that an attempt to land on the east end of the island was being made. A demolition squad stayed behind to blow up what was left of our guns.

About 0100 on May 6, 1942, the order came from our Battery Commander, Major Glassburn, for us to report at once to the Commanding Officer West Sector at Middleside Tunnel, prepared as infantry to act in beach defense reserve. I did not get to change into my clean clothes with my Bible that I had previously buried. Being a BAR man, I got my gun, ammo clips and a bandolier of hand grenades. I moved out with the battery in three platoons: two rifle platoons and one machine gun platoon. The route of our march was up Cheney Road to Battery B; down the path on the south of Topside's Parade Ground where a few months ago we marched in review before General MacArthur as he returned to active duty to take command; past the ruins of the Corregidor Cinema and Topside Barracks; down the golden stairs to Middleside; and, up Middleside's back road to the tunnel. No artillery barrage was encountered, although several were being laid down below Topside. Some large caliber tracers passed over my head as we passed the Topside Parade Ground, and seemed to be coming from Malinta Hill or beyond. Rifle and machine gun bullets were heard occasionally, but all of us reached the Middleside tunnel safely. If anyone had been afraid to face the expected hand-to-hand fighting, he could have easily disappeared into the dark in a dozen places on the way down to Middleside. All of us were eager for the encounter and none failed. Surrender was never an option for me! I didn't think about it or dwell upon it. Every day was confronted as it came – with optimism that I would see it through until the next day. Still, I was scared. Was now the time that I was going to die? What we had all dreaded was near. I crouched with the men through the heavy artillery fire hoping we wouldn't be hit. Then, a shell exploded by me. I was hit and dazed by flying rocks and shrapnel. When I finally came to, I was in the tunnel at Middleside.

Middleside tunnel was crowded. The tunnel constructed in haste was incomplete and there were several hundred Filipinos in addition to Battery F and a company of Marines waiting in it. Some of the Filipinos were Philippine Army Air Corps troops. The crowding was such that the tunnel blower system was just barely adequate to keep the air breathable. "Sit down and remain quiet" came the order. There were two radios in the Command Post, and the other with the east end sector. About daylight, those in the C.P. heard East Sector call for help: "Send all the 30-caliber ammunition that you can spare!" A little later, another message was heard coming from where the Japs had landed: "We need more men; send us men for God's sake."

Listening to these calls for help was painfully frustrating, especially for the platoon of Marines whose buddies were on the beaches, east of Malinta Hill. Our group in Middleside Tunnel was being held in reserve for the attack expected on B Sector coming up from the beach areas of Cheney and James Ravine. Coming up the Ravine, the Japanese would have been able to split our defenses.

Men from Battery F were sent from the tunnel on a detail up to Battery Wheeler 59th CA, Battery B 60th CA, Battery F 60th CA, and Battery Cheney 59th to glean any ammunition that could be found. The shelling and bombing grew heavier above the tunnel area. Some of the sticks of bombs dropped shook dirt loose from the roof and walls of the tunnel.

At 1115 hours on May 6, 1942, an order was phoned in to destroy all material and automatic weapons, ammunition, the parts and cart for them, also communication and other radio equipment. A secret document was being prepared for our surrender at 1200 hours. This order was received with some consternation. Its validity had to be verified by calling back over a different communication system. We were not expecting the surrender to come so soon. Previous radio and visual reports had indicated that the Jap's landing on Corregidor had been pretty well contained, if not repulsed. Major Glassburn came and gave orders for us to surrender to the Japanese.

Many of us talked about trying to escape from Corregidor, but decided any attempt would be futile. Destruction of all armaments and ammunition began at once. I disassembled my BAR and scattered the parts behind the bridging of the tunnel. I also hid the grenades behind the bridging.

I will never forget the scene that followed: the tunnel and cross laterals were lighted by widely spaced light bulbs, creating an eerie twilight gloom. The men working in feverish haste looked weirdly dreamlike; some sobbed aloud, some were cursing, some were praying. The noise was tremendous. At noon, all destruction of weapons ceased. Everyone sat down to catch their breath. I wondered: What now? Death, or...? Some of the men

Malinta Tunnel lateral

stepped outside the tunnel to look around, but were quickly driven back by a flight of heavy bombers which dropped bombs on the Middleside barracks, about 600 feet from the tunnel entrance.

The bombing and shelling of Corregidor did not cease at our order to surrender. Instructions arrived by runner that all officers were to prepare themselves and their sidearms for surrender to the Japanese at the tunnel entrance; the troops were to march out, carrying their rifles in one hand, and the rifle bolts in the other; the Japs

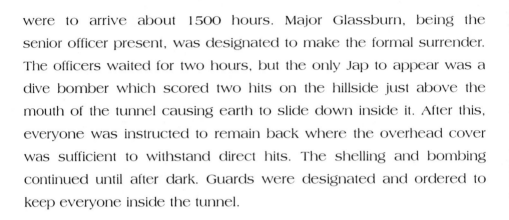

were to arrive about 1500 hours. Major Glassburn, being the senior officer present, was designated to make the formal surrender. The officers waited for two hours, but the only Jap to appear was a dive bomber which scored two hits on the hillside just above the mouth of the tunnel causing earth to slide down inside it. After this, everyone was instructed to remain back where the overhead cover was sufficient to withstand direct hits. The shelling and bombing continued until after dark. Guards were designated and ordered to keep everyone inside the tunnel.

3

A Captured Body Only

"Hell is only a state of mind; (Camp) O'Donnell was a place."
— attributed to a member of the Bataan Death March

"There are only two forces in the world, the sword and the spirit.
In the long run, the sword will always be conquered by the spirit."
– Napoleon Bonaparte

At dawn on the morning of May 7, 1942, we were still in the tunnel at Middleside. Apprehension was high. We knew that, unlike the Geneva Convention which established the rules of military captives being fed and clothed in the manner of the capturing nation's own military, the Japanese had their own beliefs. To be taken captive or surrender was a great dishonor. If not killed in battle, suicide was the next option. I had personally witnessed downed Japanese pilots being strafed by their own men to prevent them from being captured. Knowing this type of barbarity, our uncertain destiny was obvious to all of us.

Orders came for us to leave the tunnel and to proceed at once to Malinta Tunnel at Bottomside. This was the last time I saw any of the officers from Battery F. After leaving the tunnel, we encountered the Japanese at Middleside Parade Ground. We were searched for weapons and stripped of everything we had of value – watches, rings, money – everything. A Japanese soldier approached me with his

Malinta Hill *(looking south)*

General Wainwright
(surrender - 05/08/42

Japanese celebrate
fall of Corregidor

Malinta Tunnel Surrender

Surrender at Malinta Tunnel
(Everett Reamer)

Japanese search

bayonet drawn and cut off my dog tags. Low flying dive bombers caused some fear; however, they did no firing or bombing.

At approximately 0900 On May 7th, we arrived at the west entrance of Malinta Tunnel. We were herded on the North Hill just outside of the entrance. A few Jap soldiers circled around through the mob like a wild beast curiously circles its prey. They looked at us as if we were from another world. Everyone was hungry and thirsty. Eventually, some canned food was brought out of the tunnel and given to us.

Officers were taken to the entrance of the Queen's Tunnel (Navy Intercept Tunnel). At 1330 hours, the officers were ordered to proceed to the east entrance of Malinta Tunnel and assemble on the side of North Hill. As I left, I saw evidence of hand-to-hand fighting near the east end of the tunnel. Dead bodies of American defenders of Corregidor were lying on the ground everywhere. They had bloated in the sun almost beyond the point of recognition. Some had body parts missing. Others still held their weapons in firing position. At about 1500 hours, the officers were taken to Malinta Tunnel and left to their own devices. The enlisted men were on the North Hill near the west entrance of Malinta Tunnel. With Japanese cameras snapping photos of the entire scene and Japanese propaganda cameras rolling, the Japanese staff accompanied General Wainwright and his staff as they were brought out of the west end of Malinta Tunnel past us. We were ordered to hold up our hands in surrender. Many did, but not me. Not knowing my fate or future, I was in a total state of shock. Nevertheless, from my vantage point, only 40 feet away, I could see that General Wainwright's eyes were filled with tears as he looked around to see us, his head slightly bowed.

We were then marched through Malinta Tunnel to the East Road. A short distance down the road, a Jap tank had been stopped by a tank barricade firmly in place across the road. Dead bodies littered the roadway as I marched past them. The stench was terrible. Finally, we arrived at the 92nd Garage Area. Before the war, hangars for sea planes and a motor pool were located there. Because it was surrounded by hills on its other three sides, with only the southern aspect exposed, it was an ideal place for the Japanese to guard us with machine guns set on the hills above us.

Captain Thompson, a veterinary doctor who had been assigned to the hospital staff when his services were no longer needed to care for the cavalry animals, stood an impressive 6'6" tall and had a heart as big as he was. After our surrender, he expressed his concern to the Japanese for the welfare of the sick and wounded. Captain Thompson knew where food supplies were kept and insisted that he be allowed to get for the sake of these men. Another American soldier whose name was Provo had spent some time in Japan and had converted to the Shinto religion. He had found favor with the Japanese and, in their language indicated to them that Captain Thompson was a trouble-maker. The last time anyone saw Captain Thompson alive was on May 10th. He was under two Japanese guards in a captured American staff car driven by Provo. When they arrived at Kindley Field, Captain Thompson was led down over a hill out of sight while Provo remained in the car. Shots were heard. When the guards returned, Captain Thompson was not with them. Two subsequent trials have acquitted Provo; but, Captain Thompson's son, Kenneth, who is today an attorney, but who was only an infant in 1942, is still seeking justice for the loss of his father.

We had little water and no food. Catch-as-catch can, the first food I got was a can of tomatoes. I only had the clothes on my back. The first night I slept on the ground with no blanket. Later, I moved onto a concrete slab. There was only one water spigot for the entire group of approximately 6,000 men who were corralled here. We bathed in the ocean. It was a dog-eat-dog existence. The men from the various units were frustrated with the officers blaming them for our surrender. Colonel Bunker, Commander of the 59th Coastal Artillery, and who had graduated with General MacArthur from West Point, was occupying a spot immediately next to me. I had known him to be an irascibly cantankerous old bastard, but fair and honest nevertheless. He stood up and angrily stated: "This kind of bickering will not get us anywhere. Look, if we don't stand together, not one of us will make it out of here alive!" After that, the men fell silent. I never heard them complain again.

Only later would we learn that General Homma warned General Wainwright during their negotiations that he would execute all captives, disregarding them as POW's, unless there was full surrender – not only of Corregidor, but also all Americans and Filipinos still

General Homma

resisting the Japanese on other islands. This was an unimaginable violation of international convention! In the hopes of sparing the needless loss of countless lives, General Wainwright agreed.   When MacArthur was informed of Wainwright's surrender, he was furious. He immediately sent countermanding orders to fight on at all costs. These orders Wainwright ignored. He knew that to obey them would have resulted in an immediate massacre of every man, woman, and child under his authority.

I lost track of time in this moment-to-moment existence. I had plenty of time to contemplate my fate and began to develop my faith. I had to leave my Bible behind when we were forced to abandon our position on Corregidor. So, about the only scripture I could remember was the 23rd Psalm:

The Lord is my Shepherd; I shall not want.
He maketh me to lie down in green pastures.
He leadeth me beside the still waters.
He restoreth my soul.
He leadeth me in the paths of righteousness for His name's sake. Yea, though I walk through the valley of the shadow of death, I will fear no evil, for Thou art with me.
Thy rod and Thy staff they comfort me.
Thou preparest a table before me in the presence of
mine enemies.
Thou anoinest my head with oil; my cup runneth over.
Surely goodness and mercy shall follow me all the days of my life; and, I will dwell in the house of the Lord forever.

It became my greatest comfort.

On May 23rd, we were moved from the 92nd Garage Area without provisions. We moved along the South Road to the South Dock at Bottomside. At approximately 1600 hours, we were transported to a ship in the South Channel and boarded it. We slept on the deck that night still without provisions. At approximately 1000 hours May 24th, the ship moved into Manila Bay and dropped anchor just off shore in Manila Harbor. Landing craft were alongside; rope nets were thrown over the side of the ship. We climbed down the rope nets and onto the landing craft. The landing craft then departed the ship and headed for shore. They stopped short of the shore and forced us to get off into the water. We then were assembled on Dewey Boulevard, wet, hungry, thirsty.

At approximately 1500 hours, we were marched down Dewey Boulevard guarded by Japanese cavalrymen riding up and down the column. Both sides of Dewey Boulevard were lined with Filipino people. They attempted to give us food and water. When they were caught doing this, they were severely beaten by the Japanese. We ourselves were so weak we could hardly stand. The weakest of us stumbled and were cuffed back into line until they dropped.

As we marched, I looked to my left and on the grass against a

tree sat Colonel Bunker. At the time, he was 58 years old, and had succumbed to complete exhaustion. I had thought that Colonel Bunker died on this day, but after the war I learned that he had died in a Japanese prison camp on Formosa.

Bilibid Prison

After two hours had passed, we arrived at Bilibid Prison. It was beginning to get dark. I got no food but some water. Again, I slept on the ground. At approximately 0600 hours May 25, 1942, we reassembled and were marched to the Manila train yards. We were put on a train of old 40 x 8 style boxcars, so named because the cars were designed to hold either 40 men, or 8 horses. They crammed us in 100 to a boxcar with the door closed.

Bilibid Prison Hospital

The conditions were terrible. Many were sick with dysentery and malaria. The heat was horrendous. Others were still wounded without the benefit of medical attention. Many died from exhaustion and suffocation.

At approximately 1600 hours, we arrived at Cabanatuan and were removed from the train. We marched to an area just outside the city where we were corralled in an open field enclosed with barbed wire. Some food and water were provided. The food ran out before I could get any.   It was raining as I slept on the ground. Early the following morning, food was again made available until it ran out.

We were then reassembled and started to march up a gravel road. I thought we would never reach our destination. At noon,

the weakness became almost unbearable. Repeatedly, the Japs beat the weakest and tried to make them walk. We got water from holes along the road where rainwater from the previous night had collected in the caribou tracks, tire ruts, and pot holes.

Death marchers forced to wear helmets to intensify the heat

After walking 20 kilometers, we ended up at Cabanatuan Camp #3 which was an abandoned Philippine Army site. At the Camp, we were assigned to primitive buildings with thatched roofs for housing. We slept on bays built from lumber and bamboo, some of which were only 1/2 to 1 inch thick. My back screamed!

Allied soldiers marching across Bataan

We were then placed in groups of ten and were told that if any of the ten escaped, the remaining nine would be shot. These were commonly known as "blood groups". For food, we were given a small portion of mushy rice called "lugau" twice a day. Sickness was everywhere. Many of us suffered malnutrition. Tongues were raw from the excessive saliva from constantly being hungry. Yellow jaundice and beriberi were common. The Japs would just let the men lie there and die. I too had a bad case of yellow jaundice which took quite some time for me to get over. Later, I was diagnosed with amoebic dysentery as well.

There were daily burials as death rates soared. At times, the dead would be left lying near me waiting for the rain to stop so they

Burial detail

could be buried. Some of us were assigned to work details. Several of us would be sent to cut wood for fuel. It was a great relief to get outside of the barbed wire enclosure, but the danger was high. If one member of the detail escaped, it would mean death for the rest of us.

Cabanatuan Prison hut

Torture and murder were also practiced. Some men trying to buy food from the Filipinos were caught. For three days they were tortured and then made to dig their own graves near our quarters. We were forced to watch while they were shot and buried. One soldier even watched his own twin brother shot.

Death orders were equally harsh for those Filipinos captured as well. A diary presumed to have belonged to a member of the Akatsuki

force in Manila and captured at the
eventual retaking of Manila would
include this chilling entry: "...Feb. 8
– Guarded 1,164 guerrillas newly
brought in today. Feb. 9 – Burned
1,000 guerrillas to death tonight..."

Prisoner bayoneted by Japanese

In August, the Japanese
requested each of us to fill out a questionnaire. One of the questions
asked: "What class American?" I answered: "Middle class". "What
occupation?" I answered "Baker", thinking that this would get me close
to the food supply. Wrong answer: they didn't need any bakers.
To their eyes,I looked strong, so I could still perform hard labor.

On October 3, 1942, in early morning, I was one of
approximately 2,000 men who were marched back to Cabanatuan.
The rain was pouring, and I was too sick and run down to make the
journey, but was forced to make it anyway. We were put on yet
another train, taken to Manila, and ended up at Pier Seven in late afternoon. We were fed dried fish for the first time and some rice. The following morning, we boarded a Japanese ship, the Totori Maru, off Pier
Seven in Manila. Before we boarded, the Japanese loaded the cremat-
ed remains of many of their war dead. A
white ribbon suspending a small box
around the neck cradled the remains in
front of each soldier as they marched by.

The Hellship (Brazil Maru)

Japanese troops were located
amidships and aft. We were crammed forward in the hole and on deck.
Conditions were crowded so much that I or no one else had room to
lie down.

We left Manila bound for an unknown destination. The conditions on this ship were indescribably horrible. Only two small bags of oyster crackers were given to us to eat per day. The crackers had been stored in soap boxes and tasted horribly of it. All of us had diarrhea. But, the latrines were inadequate for the number of sick men aboard. Water was very limited. Sometimes, we would stand in line all day before we would get a drink. From the ship's bridge, the Japs would amuse themselves by throwing bits of rice at us and watching us fight over it.

Midway between the Philippines and our first stop, our ship, the last one in the convoy, was attacked by an Allied submarine. A torpedo came right at us, but fell short. Another torpedo passed just to the rear of our ship. The Japanese destroyers circled about dropping depth charges. "What irony it would be," I thought, "to have lived through the Jap invasion only to be killed by my own Navy!"

A few days later, we pulled into Taipai, Formosa. There, we were stripped naked and taken off the ship where we were medically inspected and hosed down. Some of the more seriously ill were taken off the ship. Many of the Japanese soldiers also left the ship and did not return.

I was one of 2,000 of us left on board now that the Japanese soldiers had departed. This gave us more room, and we could finally move about.

Later, we left harbor and after being at sea for only one day, we dropped anchor near an island and remained there for about a week. Many POW's died there while we were anchored and were buried at sea. I became aware of how cold it was becoming.

Returning to Formosa, we departed once again from that port and went on to Pusan, Korea. It was bitterly cold. I had a severe ear infection. Becoming very despondent, I said to another soldier from Battery F: "If only I had used better judgment, I wouldn't be here." He snapped back the best advice I could have received: "You're here! Make the best of it! One day...it will all end." While anchored in Pusan, 1,600 POW's were taken from the ship. I later found out that those prisoners were taken to Mukden, Manchuria. Many of them froze to death during the winter of 1942-43.

Less than 400 of us remained onboard and proceeded to a destination still unknown. An Army colonel told us: "You've been lied to, abandoned, and mistreated; but, I promise you that I will intercede for all of you from this point forward." His attention to us was a morale builder, although I never saw him again after we docked.

On November 11, 1942, we docked at Osaka, Japan. I didn't think it could be possible, but the cold temperatures only intensified. We were taken off the ship. About 100 of us, me included, were marched over to the heart of the warehouse and dock district and were housed in a prison camp known as Osaka Camp #1. Living quarters here were much better than we had before. There were 72 of us to a room which measured 25 ft. long by 20 ft. wide. We slept on wooden bays, wooden shelves mounted three high on both the left and right with a narrow center aisle for a walkway. Later on, we were issued one, thin blanket and a small, round pillow filled with grain hulls. Regular cooked rice and sparse watery soup was given twice daily. It was said to be approximately 1500 calories a day.

Among the other prisoners of war at this camp were many British captured in Hong Kong and Singapore, a few pilots from Australia and New Zealand, and Merchant Marines from the U.S.,

Britain, China and India. Most of these were survivors off ships that had been sunk by the Germans in the South Atlantic and brought to Japan for internment. One British merchant seaman appeared in a daze next to me and kept muttering: "I can't believe this...I can't believe this... I was captured by the Germans twice during World War I, and now this...I can't believe this!" Americans, however, were in the minority. There were so many different nationalities that we nick-named the Camp "The League of Nations". Because the POW's from Guam were the first ones in the camp,

Japanese prison guards

they formed the main staff. There were others captured on Wake Island. All together, we numbered about 800. I was the only one from Battery F at this camp.

We had a permanent Japanese staff, plus a rotating Japanese guard force and a staff of guards for work details. These work details had a Japanese honcho or boss. We had an American staff commander. There was also a doctor and medic who manned the aid station under the supervision of a Japanese medic. At night, one POW would be forced to stand guard in each room. No more than one man was permitted to leave the room at any time. Japanese guards would patrol the perimeter of the camp, and they constantly patrolled inside the camp compound. A squad of guards was stationed at the main gate as well.

We worked as slave laborers unloading and loading ships and barges. In steel mills, we carried bricks, crushed rock, and tamped moulds. There were foundries too. And, in lumber yards, we carried heavy timbers on our shoulders from one end of the yard to the other.

We also worked in the docks and warehouses. We worked seven days a week. Often, we would work 14 hours straight to be able to meet the quotas set by the Japanese.

We were required to muster every morning and night. At muster, we were required to count off in Japanese only.

American prisoners -
Japanese slave labor detail

If a mistake was made counting off in Japanese, the offender would be charged then beaten.

If a POW reported he was too ill for work, the determination would have to be made by a Japanese medic. Invariably, the answer would be "SHINGOTO – Work! Work!"

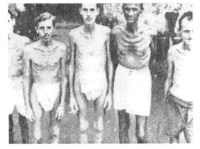

Malnutrition continued to be a problem causing night blindness. When we complained to the Japs, they didn't believe us. One night they tested us. They put timbers across a walkway and then ordered us to walk. We all stumbled and fell.

P.O.W.'s in a Japanese camp

To supplement our meager rations, we stole everything we could as often as we could on some of the work details; but, if we were caught, we were severely punished, sometimes to death. Still, we never gave up.

Also, on work details, we always tried to screw up the machinery, under cover, of course. Diesel wenches on ships could be sabotaged and were at times. Steam wenches, however, were more difficult. One time, while I was part of a detail unloading a ship of pig iron, we decided to attempt to break the steam wench by undermining the stacks of iron. We did this by forcing the net loaded with pig iron to be pulled against the entire stack. After many attempts to lift it, the Japanese signal man decided that he was going to hoist the net — no matter what! Finally, with a loud, groaning, metallic sound, the supporting mast of the ship toppled down. I looked at my work mates and quietly smiled. It was weeks before that ship returned from being repaired.

We were opposed to unloading military equipment. One day, we were ordered to unload a barge of field artillery. We refused. We were beaten – finally, after a day of stand off, the Japs relented.

Severe beatings and standing at attention without clothes in winter were common methods of punishment. One of the favorite methods of torture was to make us kneel in gravel and put a wooden stick behind our knees and between our legs. My feet were swollen; my back, raw; yet, they would yell at me, beat me, and force me on to work.

Days turned into weeks; weeks into months. I lost track of time. I felt isolated from everything familiar. No news from home, no news about the progress of the war. We knew nothing about the advances of our allied forces although, at times, ships in Osaka Harbor showed signs of having undergone attacks. Shell holes would be visible above the water line as were scorch marks from fires onboard.

I worked a Japanese army lumber yard detail. Lumber yard details were always harsh and cruel. One day, a U.S. Navy POW, Jack Leonhardt, removed his shirt. On his chest was tattooed an

American Eagle holding an American Flag. When the Japanese sergeant saw the tattoo, he lowered his head like a bull and charged repeatedly ramming the sailor and knocking him to the ground. When Jack was able to stand up again, he put his shirt back on.

In the spring of 1944, when I was working the lumber detail, some Japanese fighter planes were exercising overhead. The Japanese honcho supervising us looked skyward as the planes practiced their formations, peals, and strafing maneuvers. Brimming with arrogance, he began to brag: "You see? Mightiest air force in whole world! Greatest pilots in whole world! Our superiority shall never be defeated!" Perhaps it was my hunger or my disillusionment, but I found myself looking him directly in the eye and saying, "It won't be long before the Americans will be flying over Japan, and we'll shoot all of those planes out of the sky!" Wrong thing to say: before I knew it, the honcho picked up a 2x4, hit me across my back, and knocked me to the ground. Never again did I make such a statement. Whenever the urge arose, I would think, "Keep your thoughts to yourself, Reamer."

The lumber detail did present some opportunities that others did not. The area outside of the lumber yard was cultivated with vegetables – onions, carrots, and turnips. It was a big risk to crawl through the fence to steal them, but it was a risk we took at every opportunity. If we had been caught, we would have been shot by the guards or accused of trying to escape. Sometimes, in the yard, we would catch a snake and boil it over an open fire. We would do almost anything to get food.

Regardless of the harsh and cruel conditions, we were constantly challenging the Japanese. We criticized their crude, inefficient work methods and told them that in America those kinds of jobs would be done by automated machinery; that they couldn't expect to win a war with such outmoded methods. It was just a mild form of derision, but it kept us going and I believe is what kept most of us alive.

Sometimes on work details, we would travel through the streets of Osaka.   School children would throw stones at us. This didn't bother me too much. I was able to put myself in their shoes and understand their feelings. In general, the Japanese people were always hostile to us.   To rate the degree of their hatred, Americans were #1; British #2; Australians and New Zealanders #3; East Indians #4; and, the Chinese #5.

We all had body lice. We just couldn't get rid of them. We did have a bath house in the camp consisting of hot tubs and could bathe after a day's work. The problem was that we were given only one bar of soap every two months. There were rats in my room that roamed freely at night as we slept. Still, there was no sign of anyone from Battery F; and, being apart from my friends made it much more difficult for me.

On March 4, 1943, after almost a year in captivity, I was allowed to write a "coached" message to my family; and, a second message was allowed in 1944:

"Dear mother and all, I'm interred in Japan. My health is fair. I'm working for pay. I hope everyone at home is well and not worrying about me.   Give all the family my best regards and tell them I said "Hello". Also tell Claude and Emaline I said "Hello".   I will say good-bye for now. With much love, From your son, Everett D. Reamer"

During the entire time of my captivity, I never received one word or package from my family or anyone else, even though many attempts were made to send them.

But, later in the spring of 1943, I was approached by a fellow POW who had been serving in the Philippines. Cautiously looking about, he said, "I think this belongs to you." There, in his outstretched hand, was my khaki-covered New Testament! I was speechless! What were the chances of that Bible which I had buried ever being found and returned to me? Under the circumstances and after all this time, it was unbelievable! The inscription that Aunt Ida had written so long ago about loneliness, despair, and hope was almost prophetic!

In the spring of 1944, a Marine who had been captured on Wake Island lay dying near me. One night, he became incoherent and kept talking to his mother, saying: "The war is over, Mom. We'll be coming home soon." He died the following day. In another incident, a young soldier from Arkansas started to swell up. He was dead in two days. It was easy to die. All you had to do was give up. After you gave up, it usually took only about ten days for a man to die.

In August 1944, we had not received any Red Cross supplies for a year. In all the time before that, I had received only two issues of the food parcels; and, at each issue, the parcel would be split between four of us, although the Red Cross had intended the whole parcel to be distributed to only one man. We knew the Japs were helping themselves to the supplies because the Supply Room was in front of our quarters. Furthermore, they had told us that, if any of us were seen around the Supply Room, we would be shot.

We were starved, so six of us decided to take action. We drew straws to see who would go to the Supply Room and bring out a Red Cross box. You might know I would be the one to draw the short straw. Another soldier, Lewis J. Bradshaw from Ralston, Oklahoma, drew the next shortest and was chosen to stand guard in our room. Since the Japs allowed only one man out of the room at a time after dark, our man would check each person as he went out and check him in again before any other person was allowed to leave the room.

The Jap guards made their rounds every few minutes. After one of them made his usual round, Bradshaw went to turn out the lights while I stood guard for him. When he returned, I left the room and unlocked the storehouse with a key another of us had made and got three of the boxes out, taking them to an adjacent latrine. Everything was going according to plan until the Jap guards saw the lights were out in the storehouse. There was yelling as the guards ran toward the area. I left the food parcels in the latrine, locked the door, and climbed over the top into another latrine.

While the guards were in a huddle, I made my way past them back to my room. As I entered the room, I could hear a guard running behind me. I crawled into my sleeping space on the top bay and pretended to be asleep. I was scared. I knew it was certain death if caught. The Japs looked everyone over. They had searched the latrine and found the Red Cross box. Bradshaw was still standing guard and when he refused to tell them who had entered the room, they began to kick and slap him around.They said they would punish the whole room if they didn't find out who did it. Finally, they left.

Beginning the next morning, all food was cut off to our room. We were told that there would be none until the culprits were discovered. I felt terrible that my fellow POW's were being starved.

Bradshaw and I went to the American Camp Commander, Chief Boatswain Mate Sanders. We told what we had done asking if he would intercede on our behalf. Sanders led me to believe that he could get the problem taken care of and get our food rations restored. But, in truth, he was not anxious to help as the Japs always gave him cuts out of the Red Cross food supplies. Our highest ranking non-commissioned officer in camp went to Sanders and told him that, if he turned us over to the Japanese, they would see that he got a court martial when the war was over.

The following morning while in line for our work detail, Bradshaw and I were called out and taken before the Japanese Camp Commander. Taken back into camp, we were both questioned. We both admitted that we were the only ones involved in the incident.

The Japanese guards started beating us: first with their fists, then with their open hands across our face. More questions. Then, the officer picked up a wooden name plate from a desk and beat us across the face with it. Not through, he then got a leather belt and beat us across the face and body with it. When we fell to the floor, they'd beat us back to our feet. Then, this same officer made us hold an office chair over our heads for two hours. He said that this was Japanese Army punishment. When Bradshaw and I would weaken and lower our arms, we would be beaten again across our arms with a bamboo pole.

I was bruised and my mouth was bleeding. Bradshaw had a deep wound down the side of his jaw. All of the Japs in the office were quite amused. Then, they pushed us outside in front of the guard house by the gate going into camp. As the Japs would pass us, they would kick us or hit us. We were still holding the chairs over our heads, not daring to lower our arms.

Sore, weak, and sick, we finally were allowed to put the chairs down. They tried to get me to produce the key to the storehouse. Unsuccessful in their attempts, they made Bradshaw and I stand at attention in front of the guardhouse.

They took Bradshaw in around one o'clock in the afternoon. Much later, when he came out, he was soaked from head to foot. They had given him the "water treatment". Then it was my turn. The guards took me in and tied me face up to a bench. Then, they asked me all sorts of questions as they slapped and pounded me. Then, the "water treatment" began: they took a fire extinguisher and forced the hose down my throat. They then pumped water into my lungs. They kept pumping and pumping until I thought I was a goner. Finally, my body recoiled, letting go full force all the pressure the water had created. It soaked the Japanese officer above me. Enraged, he beat me across the face and roughly pushed me back to the front of the guard house.

Bradshaw and I stood at attention for the rest of that day and night.   As Wednesday dawned, I felt myself slump, only to be awakened by the "crack" of a bamboo pole swung painfully against my back. "You stand at attention!" shouted my guard. "You fail, you die!" he growled. As night came, the cold and damp saturated us making every breath a stinging insult to my irritated lungs.

Thursday would bring the August sun and a heat that seemed to roast us where we stood. No water, except for the taste of salt I licked from the corners of my mouth. Night came again with its deathly quiet, punctuated only by the sounds of the guards' boots as they walked by us, and the crashing pain of the bamboo against my back and arms. Each stroke made me catch my breath in deep, wheezing agonies.

Another morning arose with a Friday sun's new rays piercing our eyes and stinging more than the sweat that trickled into them. It coursed its own ticklish water torture down my neck and back. Every movement which met with the Japs' disapproval brought more

P.O.W.'s forced to stand
at attention

beatings, more swears, more shouts. My thighs ached, and my arms felt leaden. No food as hunger fed on me continuously, and my lips began to parch and swell.

The days were marked only by the alternating sun and moon and the passing of our POW buddies to and from their work details. As they passed, I could catch sight of their eyes and at times a squint...a furtive glance or nod...a bravely stolen wink. They knew what we were up against, and they were with us. This was a life and death struggle!

As Friday night loomed, my ears were filled with the pulsing of my own blood as I seemed to lose sense of each additional hour's passage. I was numb, but still the bamboo beatings registered on my exquisitely painful back. After a while, the pulsing in my ears was replaced by the white noise of lost reality which only seemed to be brought back to its senses by the eyes of my buddies marching past us. I had to hold on! They had faith in me. I had to have faith in myself...

The Lord is my Shepherd. I shall not want...Each morning I had promised myself nothing more than seeing my way to the next night. And, each night, I promised myself nothing more than seeing my way to the next dawn.

Saturday was upon us, but I was in no way aware of it....still no water...no food...we stood in our own filth.   Heat with its malicious sweat and steam kept trying to beat us down. Cold with its mocking dew and clamminess kept defying our ability to stand still. The pain still made its bamboo impression, but somehow it was becoming more distant.

By Sunday, I had become a zombie. My ankles were swollen three times their normal size such that I could hardly stand. My face was swollen, bruised, and bleeding; and, my back was raw and oozing blood. Thirst, hunger, sight, hearing – all my senses seemed to be fading into a single gray haze. Then, on Sunday night, as the Japanese Camp Commander started the evening muster of all POW's, and the guards were called to attention, I passed out. When I collapsed, some British POW's rushed to me and challenged the Jap guards who were preparing to execute me as they had promised. Those same British soldiers carried me to their room where I stayed over night; but, I never knew I was there.

When I came to the next morning, I was in a triangular room under Japanese guard. Bradshaw was also in the room. It was a very small brig with just enough room to lie down. There was also a Hindu prisoner in the room who had gone insane. His insanity, however, did not free him from the indignities of torture. The guard would force him to masturbate and then would burn him on the head of his penis with cigarettes. He had to use the floor for a latrine and would sleep in it. The stench was sickening. These indignities were not forced upon Bradshaw and me, but we were forced to watch and endure them.

They began to feed us again, starting with 1/4 bowl of rice in the morning and another in the evening. The ration was later increased to 1/2 bowl.

About 0630 to 0730 hours in the morning, they would put us at the front gate in front of the camp guards, tie our hands behind our backs, and force us to stand in the sun. While we were out there, Bradshaw and I saw them take one Red Cross parcel and give it to an American doctor for distribution to the men who were sick. Recall that a box of Red Cross food was only supposed to be for one man. The doctor had to split it between 15 or more sick men. The doctor would also have to argue with the Japs to get them to not force a man with a high fever to work. I also saw two more food parcels being taken into Jap headquarters by the Japanese Camp Commander.

On September 17, 1944, after a month of this day-in day-out existence, we had a typhoon. Water was still standing in the streets on the next day, when Bradshaw and I were forced to march in waist-deep water for over a mile. Our hands were tied behind our backs with rope. Our guards took off their shoes, tied the laces and hung them about our necks. Under these armed guards we were forced to march across town. When we finally came to dry ground, our guards put their boots back on, but we continued to march barefoot. While walking, we came face to face with two German sailors. One was as red-headed as I was and the other blonde. When they looked at us, they started to laugh. I will never forget those bastards! I wanted to kill them!

Finally, at midday, we came to Chumegoome, Japanese Army Headquarters. We were forced to sign papers, written in Japanese, without knowing their content. We waited there all morning. Even so, we were not given any food or water.

In the afternoon, we were called before a military court to be judged by three Japanese military officers. Given no defense counsel, a Jap from our camp was assigned as an interpreter, although he could hardly speak English. The three military judges asked us many questions and inquired how we liked Japan and who we thought would win the war. "Naturally, I am an American," I told them, "and I think that America will win the war." They laughed.

Bradshaw and I tried to explain why we took the Red Cross food parcels. We told them that we saw the Japs helping themselves to the supplies intended for us. Our interpreter could not – or would not – tell them what we were saying.

After they deliberated, the judge stated through the interpreter, "I sentence you to one year solitary confinement." He asked me: "What do you think about that?" I said, "I don't think it's fair because we only attempted to take what was ours to begin with."

Our hands were cuffed behind our backs with a rope attached to the handcuffs for them to lead us. A hood was placed over our head to blindfold us. I was thinking that blindfolded men were usually beheaded – or were they going to shoot us? We were escorted out of the building. I thought we were taking our last steps. They put us on a train. That evening, we got off the train and walked for a mile or so.

When our hoods were finally removed, we were inside Osaka Sakai Military Prison, an edifice of brick surrounded by a 15 foot high wall. At the prison receiving center, they stripped us of everything, including my Bible with which I had been reunited. We were given a red shirt and pants that looked like cheesecloth. We had no underwear and no shoes. They then gave us a small bowl of rice to eat.

We were then taken to a cell block by way of the highest catwalk. Separating Bradshaw and me, we were put one to a cell. With a cell dimension of 5 x 7 ft., there was just room enough to lie down with only the bare, wooden floor to sleep on. There was one, thin blanket padded with cotton which had shifted all to one side. There were no sanitary facilities except for a wooden bucket and small wash basin; no heat; and no running water. A barred, four pane, open window at the rear end of the cell 6 feet from the floor let in the cold air. My clothing was not sufficient to keep me warm. A single light bulb hung from the ceiling and burned day and night. The walls were solid masonry and the cell door was solid wood with a small screened slot at eye level through which the guards could see inside the cell without being seen themselves. Next to the cell door was a small pass-through for food and water which itself also had a latched exterior door.

I can still hear the click of the cell door as it locked behind me. I had never felt such isolation! I was completely alone. I wondered: "What now? Will this be the end for me?"

There were seven other military POW's confined to solitary at this prison. Besides myself, there were two British soldiers who had been sentenced to life imprisonment for an escape; a Dutch national, Gerre De Vos, who was serving a three year sentence for hitting a Japanese worker. He had fought and was captured by the Japanese on Java. There were also four other Americans: Ben Magden of the 31st Infantry who had been captured on Bataan. He became insane before the end of the war. They had taken all his food from him and at his release he was nothing but skin and bones. Robert Newton was a Marine captured on Guam and sentenced to 18 months for stealing sugar from a warehouse. Francis L. Joslin from Missoula, Montana had been with the 59th Coastal Artillery on Corregidor at Fort Hughes. The Japs accused him of attempting an escape. Although he denied it, he was sentenced to one year of solitary. He was tried and sentenced at the same time Bradshaw and I were. And, then, of course, there was Lewis J, Bradshaw of the 59th CA at Fort Hughes Corregidor.

There were also eight civilians confined to solitary: one French, two Dutch, two Russians and two Germans who were all accused of espionage and one unidentified national by the name of Mike Bonifer.

My food consisted of 1/4 bowl of rice and about the same amount of water. Food rations were categorized in a range from 1 to 7, with #1 being the largest, and #7 the smallest. I was placed on #7 rations — only 500 calories per day. When they fed me my small portion of rice, I had to kneel to eat it. Regardless of the range, we continued to be hungry. One day, we were taken from our cells and forced to make canteen holders. They said if we did not make them, we would not even get that little bit of rice to eat. My weight had gone from 160 lbs. at the time of my capture to about 120 lbs. by the time I was placed in solitary confinement.

We were not permitted to talk to anyone. There was never anything with which to occupy our time. Once every two weeks – sometimes just once a month – I along with the others were permitted to walk in a circle five or ten minutes. We were not permitted to exercise or stand up in our cell. We could only sit upright. The order to retire would come about 2100 hours at which time we could lie down for the night. Our wake up order came about 0700 hours. We were mustered in the morning and the night. The guard would call out the cell number through the screen slot in the door.

The prisoner would respond with his prison number. My prison number was "ichisen gobeyoko hatchiju ku" (# 1589).

I was permitted to bathe only once a month. The bathing facility consisted of three 50-gallon oil drums, tops removed and filled with water over an open fire pit. Each of us would climb into the first drum and get wet. From the second drum, we would dip out a small pail of water which we used to bathe our bodies. Finally, we would climb into the third drum for the final rinse. After our bath, we would be marched naked back to our cells. Fleas were a constant problem, yet entertaining. The cells were so quiet that when the fleas jumped I could hear them.

While exercising in the prison yard in November, one of the civilian prisoners who was bilingual reported that the war was closing in as the Allied landings were occurring in the Marianna Islands.

In December, one of the Dutch civilians in a cell directly on the other side of my own died. I was told that he had been the Governor General of Dutch East Indies. I also learned after the war that during December in Alongapo Harbor, P.I., American POW's were being moved out of the Philippines as quickly as possible to Japan to be used as possible bargaining chips in negotiating favorable terms for the Japanese. The Oryoko Maru was loaded mostly with officers and some enlisted men. U.S. planes attacked the unmarked ship and sunk it. Among the many American POW's who died was my Battery F Commander, Major Robert Glassburn. Still, some managed to get ashore where they ended up on a tennis court. When the survivors were questioned by the Japanese, they were asked who among them were too sick or ill to travel. Some 20 men stated that they were. That evening, those same men were escorted by the Japanese to a secluded hillside out of the sight of observation, or so they thought. Two Filipinos, however, hidden from view, secretly watched as Japanese soldiers repeatedly charged the men with bayonets until they were all dead. The others who had been left back at the tennis court were placed on another ship and transported to Japan where they remained until the end of the war.

The winter of 1944-45 was one of Japan's coldest. By December, the weather had turned the bitterest of cold. Since we had no heat or warm clothing, it was a challenge each day to stay warm. And, because we were fed so little, our bodies could hardly generate enough heat to prevent us from freezing to death. My health as well as my weight continued to decline. Because there was snow on the ground, our monthly exercise program was discontinued, but we were allowed to continue our monthly baths. I tried to get medical treatment for my back since it was still raw from the beatings and wounds. When I would yell for help, they would unlock the wooden door to my cell; then, when I told them I needed medical attention, the guards would shove me back into my cell and lock the door again.

This kept on until January of 1945. By then, my right hand was now frozen. I'd try to put it under my left arm to keep it warm, but finally the pain became too intense. As my condition worsened, I knew I had to do something to get attention. Since lying down was against the rules, I decided that lying down was what I would do. All day and all night, I lay on the floor, too sick to move. The guards would open the cell door, now and then, and beat me and kick me. "I need a doctor," I would groan. The Jap guard would tell me that I wasn't sick. My right hand kept swelling and extended all the way to my elbow. I thought I was going to lose my hand and likely my arm. I couldn't even get my shirt over it. My hand, now twice its normal size,

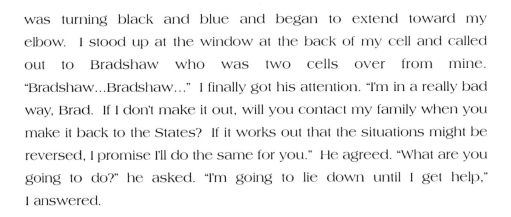

was turning black and blue and began to extend toward my elbow. I stood up at the window at the back of my cell and called out to Bradshaw who was two cells over from mine. "Bradshaw...Bradshaw..." I finally got his attention. "I'm in a really bad way, Brad. If I don't make it out, will you contact my family when you make it back to the States? If it works out that the situations might be reversed, I promise I'll do the same for you." He agreed. "What are you going to do?" he asked. "I'm going to lie down until I get help," I answered.

After four days of my lying down, the guards continuing their usual pattern of kicking and yelling for me to get up, I heard a voice through the inspection vent of my cell speaking perfect English: "What is your problem?". I spoke through the door and told him of the condition of my hand, arm and feet – that they were frozen and infected. He called a guard to come and unlock the cell. When the door opened, he explained that he was the warden of the prison. He ordered them to get me to the doctor at the dispensary. Even though my feet were frozen, I had to walk barefoot through the snow to the dispensary approximately 1.5 miles away.

When we reached the dispensary, they put me on a bench, lying on my back, with my hands over my head. The doctor did not give me anything to put me to sleep, but went ahead and lanced my hand between my thumb and forefinger and scraped it. The pain was so bad, I screamed and screamed. I bet they could hear me all over the prison. He then packed the one inch deep wound with medicated gauze. I was given nothing for pain. My toes were raw. I pointed to them and asked for medication. He just dabbed a bit of salve on top of them, and I was forced to walk back to my cell through the snow.

They changed the bandage on my hand about every other day. There were permission slips written in Japanese which told me when to go back to the doctor. I was supposed to have it renewed, but I did not know enough Japanese to understand it and was too sick to care. So, when I went back for a bandage change, there were two young Jap prisoners who were assigned to the dispensary as medical assistants. I was asked if I could read Japanese. I said that I could not, but he told me that I could. One of them picked up a hard pole about 4 feet long and started beating me. He beat me to my knees and then started to dead-drop the pole on top of my head. I though my head would burst. Two big lumps arose on my head for over a month afterwards and my head ached for a longer time after that. But, I swore I would never go back to the dispensary for help again.

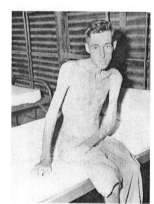

P.O.W. in Japanese
Camp Hospital

Later, in March, the weather began to warm and we were able to resume our exercise program in the prison yard. From the civilian prisoners who could speak and understand Japanese, we learned that the war was getting closer and closer. The Philippines had been retaken, and the Mariannas were now occupied by American forces. This wonderful news lifted our spirits.

In April, the announcement came over the prison's public address system 'ROOSEVELTO SENDAI" – President Roosevelt – dead! The Japanese started shouting "BANZAI!" " BANZAI!" This was the best news they had heard because they thought that the President's death assured their victory. They believed that with the loss of our leader, the war would end and they would be victorious. Perhaps they held this belief because they thought their own Emperor Hirohito was a god. Everything the Japanese did, they did for their Emperor. It was understandable that they would believe Americans would no longer pursue the war after the loss of their "god".

Their relief didn't last long as the Americans started to drop bombs over Tokyo, Osaka, and other key cities in April. Whenever the air raid siren sounded, they would cuff our hands behind our backs and leave us in our cells. It became quite an effort for the guards to keep doing this as the air raids became more and more frequent and more intense.

F.D.R.'s funeral procession

I kept losing weight; I couldn't sleep at night. My mind would go blank for hours at a time. When I would come to, I'd find myself beating my fist against the cell, banging my head, and screaming. I would snap myself out of it and pray to God to help me. I recalled the inscription on Aunt Ida's Bible and believed that its return had been nothing short of a miracle to help me hold on day by excruciating day.

The cell was full of fleas, body lice, and bed bugs. Because of malnutrition, I had become even more night blinded. Lights looked blue to me. I couldn't see at night when our planes came over on their bombing runs. I started praying that they would hit me. This was my lowest point. It was

Japanese bowing to Hirohito's Imperial Palace

Emperor Hirohito

mid-May and I had nearly given up. My rice portion kept getting small-er. I pounded on the cell floor and told the guards that the Jap "trusties" were taking half of my rice. He threatened to cut my head off if I did not shut up. He would pull his sword from its sheath and wave it over my head. He said I'd be killed before the Americans took me back.

We got only 1/2 cup of water a day. In the winter, it was ice cold; in summer, it was so hot you could hardly drink it. They also clipped all the hair off my head. We had no soap or adequate water to wash with in the cell. We didn't know what a toothbrush was. Finally, by June, 1945, my toes, hand, and back healed.

P.O.W. Execution

One day, when they gave me my small portion of rice, the pass-through door to my cell was left unlatched, and I was able to see that the amount of rice given to the Japanese prisoners was much larger than I was receiving. I became infuriated and threw my meager portion back through the portal. It scattered on the walkway outside my cell. I began to pound on the wooden cell door and yell. The guard came, unlocked my cell door and pulled me out of my cell. A Jap officer came and I told him that they were starving me to death, that I didn't have enough food to survive on and that they would have to answer for my mistreatment and starvation when the Americans came. He became enraged and knocked me to the floor and started to wave his sword over my head, telling me that I would never see the day that the Americans would re-take me. He then shoved me back into my cell, closed, and locked the door.

Near the end of June with the air raids intensifying over Japan, one of the German civilian prisoners began to pound on his cell door, yelling "Why don't you Japanese give up? You've lost the war." He kept yelling over and over. I heard the guards rush to his cell. I could hear them beating him as he kept screaming until they finally beat him senseless.

By now, the air raids were so frequent that our exercise in the yard stopped; and, in early July, the guards stopped their practice of handcuffing us with each air raid siren. I was relieved to think that if a bomb did hit the prison now, I could probably dig my way out.

For the third time in my solitary confinement, I was moved — this time to cell #13. I could sense that things were beginning to get worse. The Japanese guards were becoming even harsher and their attitude toward me colder. Food was barely a mouthful. From the back window of my cell, I could see

American bombers

planes. They were marked with a white star with slashes to the right and left of the star. What foreign planes are these I asked myself? Russian, or...whose? I didn't realize they were our own American planes. Our insignia had been changed. The star in the heart of a red circle had been removed to avoid mistaking them for Japan's rising sun insignia.

On August 6 and 9, 1945, atomic bombs were dropped on Hiroshima and Nagasaki. Hirohito's reign was coming to an end. The Japanese military high command advised him to surrender under the best possible terms. If the atomic bombs had not been dropped,

President Harry S. Truman

if a full-scale invasion of the Japanese mainland had occurred, we would have been put to death by virtue of an earlier circulated order

which read: "...extreme measures to be taken against all POW's; i.e., whether they are destroyed individually or in groups, or however it is done – with mass bombing, poisonous smoke, poisons, drowning, decapitation or what – dispose of the prisoners as the situation dictates. In any case, it is the aim not to allow the escape of a single one, to annihilate them all and not to leave any traces..." The high command's order to surrender nullified this order. President Truman's decision to drop the

Paul Tibbets prior to take-off to drop atomic bomb

atomic bombs had literally saved me and us all from an undeniably certain death.

On August 22, 1945, after months of torturous conditions, something extraordinary occurred. It was at the evening mealtime. I had received a huge bowl of rice. That was so very unusual that I was shocked. I had just started to dig in with my chopsticks, when the cell was abruptly unlocked and opened. A guard motioned for me to come out. I refused to leave that bowl of rice uneaten – for what? The guard then

Atomic bomb drop - Hiroshima

came and pulled me out of the cell. When I was outside, I noticed that the seven other POW's confined to solitary were all lined up in the center of the cell block. I thought maybe all the rice they had given me was intended to be a last supper before execution. We were marched to the center of the cell block to the control desk. It was at this time that I noticed that behind the guard station, the Japanese flag encased in a frame had been turned face to the wall. This was unusual. Something big had happened. We were escorted to a meeting room; and, to our surprise, there were two Japanese officers, along with an interpreter, there to meet us.

General Wainwright observing General MacArthur signing surrender

General Umezu signs instrument of surrender for Japanese

The Japanese officers, speaking in Japanese, and interpreted for us in English said: "The war is now over. We are now friends." They extended their hands to us in a friendly gesture, but we refused to shake them. Up until this moment, I had been 11 months and 4 days in solitary – overall, I had been a POW for 1,218 days.

We were then escorted to the Prison Administration section and the medical center where we were weighed and given Japanese army uniforms and shoes. I weighed 92 lbs. We were taken from the prison and put on a Japanese army truck, four on each side of the truck bed facing each other. As we came to the city of Osaka, all I saw was devastation. Bodies were everywhere, some lying by the

Liberated P.O.W.'s in Japan

roadside covered with sheet metal. Bradshaw must have felt some vindication when he saw the destruction because he could no longer contain himself. Pointing at the dead bodies, he yelled: "You bastards got what you deserved!" The Jap officers escorting us looked straight ahead with somber expression. Elbowing Bradshaw I said quietly, "Brad, don't screw it up now! We've come through too much!"

The Japanese officers transported us to an area close to where Osaka Camp #1 had been. But, while we were in solitary, my camp had been bombed and burned to the ground. There was nothing to come back to. My original group had been moved to another camp somewhere inland. There were a few Americans still there, but they were in dire circumstances. Sergeant Charles Coleman, who everyone had called P-40 for the type of plane he flew, told me that as the camp was bombed and burning, he sat and watched it go up in smoke and ash, clapping his hands and joyously shouting, "Burn you, S.O.B., burn!"

I then started to search for other Americans. Bradshaw and I talked our way onto a train. The Japanese were now very courteous to us, bowing and stepping out of our way. We finally ended up in Kobe, Japan and found a large group of Americans who had been held as POWs. They were camped out in an old burned-out school house. The Frenchman whom I had met in Sakai Prison was married to a Japanese woman and had a home outside of Kobe. He came to this location and invited both Bradshaw and me to go to his beach home where he provided good food and shelter for us. His wife treated us very well too, cooking for us; preparing our beds; and, doing our laundry. Mike Bonifer also came to the camp and gave Bradshaw and me several hundred Yen to spend. We were with our French host only a few days. Because he had a short wave radio, he knew about the formal surrender and the whereabouts of recovery teams coming into Kobe.

Going back to the camp at the school house, near the end of August 1945, American C-45 planes began to parachute food and medical supplies to us. Food, finally food! Did I ever eat well! Despite the warnings not to overeat, I got hives from how rich real food again was.

On September 6, 1945, a contingency from the First Cavalry Division came to Kobe camp. All of us Americans were examined to determine who needed immediate treatment and what mode of transportation was needed to evacuate them. They determined that my physical problems were severe. I was directed to be shipped by train to the Hospital Ship Marigold in Yokahama Bay. In leaving, I also had to leave Bradshaw behind. Regretfully to this day, I have never seen him again, despite my determined efforts to locate him back in the States.

After spending a few days on the Marigold, I was transported by ambulance to Atsugi Air Base near Tokyo and placed on a C-54 hospital plane and flown to the 148th General Hospital on Saipan. While there, I attended the first movie I had seen since 1941 on Corregidor. My first two purchases were a Bulova watch and a fountain pen. I was interviewed by a correspondent from Time Magazine, but I think my statements were censored by the Army as they were never published. After approximately two weeks on Saipan, I convinced the doctors I was well enough to go home. I was flown to Hickham Field in Hawaii and then back to Letterman General Hospital in San Francisco.

As I flew over the Golden Gate Bridge, I recalled sailing under it on March 31, 1941 aboard the *USAT Republic* bound for the Philippines. And, as I looked north out the window of my hospital plane, I saw a formation of white rocks on the hillside. They spelled out "WELCOME HOME". What a glorious sight indeed!

My Aunt Ida visited me while I was at Letterman. I told her the story of the loss and return of my New Testament; and, that I believed the message of hope she had promised I would find had given me the strength to endure the horror and brutality I experienced at the hands of the Japanese. It was also here that I was officially debriefed by the Army and allowed to make my first telephone call home.

After a few weeks in San Francisco, I was placed on a hospital train and transported to Fletcher General Hospital in Cambridge, Ohio, the nearest military hospital to my family home in Cleves. Before my arrival in Cambridge in October, I was able to get a 10-day delay in route to visit my mother and family whom I had not seen for over four and one-half years. It was a joyful reunion for us all!

In January 1946, I was transferred to Percy Jones Hospital in Battle Creek, Michigan. I was then sent to Fort Sheridan in Illinois where, on November 11, 1946, I was honorably discharged from the Army and given funds which allowed me to finally return home. Home! My home! Sweet, sweet home! My prisoner of war experience was over! Thank God!

American National Cemetery *(Manilla)*

Everett Reamer receiving decoration from Ambassador
to the Philippines

Everett and his wife Bernice at Topside Memorial
dedication *(05/06/02)*

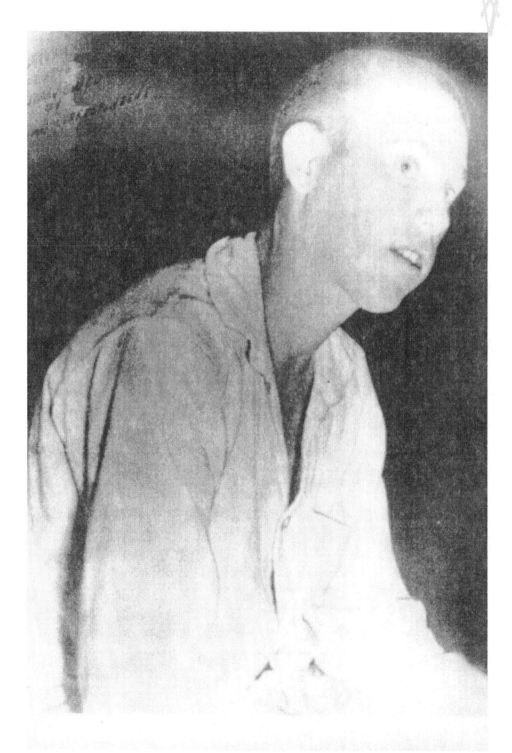

Everett after liberation *(148th Hospital)*

About the Author

Everett D. Reamer was honorably discharged from the U.S. Army as a Corporal and was the recipient of 2 Purple Hearts and a Bronze Star with 3 Presidential Citations.

Upon his return to civilian life, he served as a Maintenance Supervisor for National Steel and a Production Supervisor for General Motors. In addition, he served as Vice-Chairman of the Planning and Zoning Commission of Allen Park, Michigan.

He is the author of <u>Sanity Gone Amuck</u> and is a much sought after speaker and is featured in numerous news and magazine articles. In 1992, he was the subject of an "ABC Nightly News" special on the 50th anniversary of the fall of Corregidor. Additionally, he is listed in The Guiness Book of World Records for being forced to stand motionless during his 132 hours of torture.

Presently, Everett is Commander of the Western States Chapter of the Defenders of Bataan and Corregidor. He is a member of North Bend Lodge #346 Free and Accepted Masons. A member of the Ancient Accepted Scottish Rite, he was created a Sovereign Grand Inspector General, 33rd Degree, Honorary Member of that body's Supreme Council; and, was the keynote speaker of "The Heroes of a Generation Class" of the Valley of Cincinnati in April of 2004. Moreover, he has served as the President of the Congregation, as well as Finance Chairman of St. John's United Church of Christ in Delhi, Ohio.

He is married to Bernice Cole Reamer. They have a son, Everett C. Reamer; a daughter, Melissa C. Reamer; and, share three daughters, Betty, Violet, and Marjorie, from a previous marriage.

Currently retired, Everett and Bernice divide their time between their homes in Cleves, Ohio and Lake Havasu City, Arizona.

About the Editor

John M. Cutter is the author of the plays, "Nightmare House: Truman at Potsdam"; "Monuments of Our Future"; "A Lamp Shining Still"; and, "Brother Harry", as well as the Cable-TV script, "Rose of Sharon".

With numerous other professional publications and presentations to his credit, he practices as a family and laser-assisted dentist in Fairfield, Ohio.

Unconquerable Faith
ORDER FORM

SHIP TO:

Name _____

Address_____

City _____

State _____Zip _____

Email _____

Telephone ( ) _____

TO ORDER,
complete a copy of this
order form and mail it along
with your check or money
order payment to:
Fly Paper Productions
Publishing Group
Box 324
Harrison, OH 45030 USA

ISBN	PRODUCT	QUANTITY	UNIT PRICE	TOTAL
0-9724397-2-2	Printed Book		$24.00 US $32.95 CN	$

Check here if you
would like your book
autographed by the
author.

7% Ohio Sales Tax
(Ohio Residents Only)

GRAND TOTAL

Prices include shipping & handling. Make your check or
money order Payable to *Fly Paper Productions*. Allow
14 days for delivery. *CN indicates Canadian pricing.*